To Keith,
Dare to Dream God's
dream!

[signature]

DARE TO DREAM

Also by Mike Slaughter

shiny gods

Christmas Is Not Your Birthday

Change the World

Spiritual Entrepreneurs

Real Followers

Momentum for Life

UnLearning Church

Upside Living in a Downside Economy

MIKE SLAUGHTER

DARE TO DREAM

CREATING A GOD-SIZED MISSION STATEMENT FOR YOUR LIFE

Abingdon Press
Nashville

Dare to Dream:
Creating a God-Sized Mission Statement
for Your Life

by Mike Slaughter

Copyright © 2013 by Abingdon Press
All rights reserved.

This book is printed on acid-free, elemental chlorine-free paper.
ISBN 978-1-4267-7577-2

Scripture quotations unless noted otherwise are from the Common English Bible. Copyright © 2011 by the Common English Bible. All rights reserved. Used by permission. www.CommonEnglishBible.com.

Scripture quotations marked KJV are from The Authorized (King James) Version. Rights in the Authorized Version in the United Kingdom are vested in the Crown. Reproduced by permission of the Crown's patentee, Cambridge University Press.

Scripture quotations marked (NIV) are taken from the Holy Bible, New International Version®, NIV®. Copyright © 1973, 1978, 1984, 2011 by Biblica, Inc.™ Used by permission of Zondervan. All rights reserved worldwide. www.zondervan.com. The "NIV" and "New International Version" are trademarks registered in the United States Patent and Trademark Office by Biblica, Inc.™

Scripture quotations marked NLT are taken from the Holy Bible, New Living Translation, copyright © 1996, 2004, 2007. Used by permission of Tyndale House Publishers, Inc., Carol Stream, Illinois 60188. All rights reserved.

Scripture quotations marked NRSV are taken from the New Revised Standard Version of the Bible, copyright 1989, Division of Christian Education of the National Council of the Churches of Christ in the United States of America. Used by permission. All rights reserved.

13 14 15 16 17 18 19 20 21 22—10 9 8 7 6 5 4 3 2 1

MANUFACTURED IN THE UNITED STATES OF AMERICA

To our first grandson,
Luke Michael Slaughter

Contents

Prologue

How many times have you heard yourself saying, "Someday I'm going to…"? Fill in the blank.

Sound familiar? I believe that "someday" is the enemy to the gift of today. "Someday" is daydreaming. Before Jesus Christ transformed my life, I did a whole lot of daydreaming. I used to sit in school, stare out the window, and daydream hour after hour. I had the grades to prove it. But daydreaming and God-dreaming are not the same thing. Daydreaming is putting off today what you dream of for tomorrow. God-dreaming means putting feet to faith.

I tell the people in my congregation that my job is to remind them every week that they are going to die. Now, that may not fit your perfect picture of how to win friends and influence people, but time is short! The Book of James urges us to embrace the gift of today and start experiencing no-regret living: "You don't really know about tomorrow. What is your life? You are a mist that appears for only a short while before it vanishes" (James 4:14). How much of our energy is focused on reaching our version of tomorrow, when we may drop dead before tomorrow ever arrives? James goes on to say, "It is a sin when someone knows the right thing to do and doesn't do it" (4:17).

God didn't create us to sit around waiting to die so we can leave Planet Earth and go to heaven. He created in each of us a unique God-dream for getting more heaven into Planet Earth. We need to start living the life that God created us to live.

I am so blessed that I have been given a God-dream worth living for—and dying for. It gives me the energy I need to get out of bed every morning. It gives me purpose and makes my life one continuous song of ascent. It gives me a glimpse of what Jesus meant when he said, "I am come that they may have life, and that they may have it more abundantly" (John 10:10 KJV).

Without a God-dream, it would be so easy for me to plateau. I know too many people who have gotten stuck. They hit their forties or fifties and just stop. Life for them begins to be about looking back instead of moving forward. I meet other people who are in perpetual motion but aren't going anywhere because they lack direction. Motion and direction are not synonymous. Does either of those descriptions sound like you?

I wrote *Dare to Dream* with three purposes in mind. First, I want to wake you up to the God-dream inside of you. You have one; I am sure you do. Jesus gave the dream to you when he came into your life. Second, I want to help you develop a life mission statement. You may have life goals, but that's not the same. Goals can change by season or circumstance, but a life mission statement never changes. Third, I want to challenge you to commit fully to your God-directed life mission, starting now. Remember, you are going to die. Today is the day to seize the present of the presence.

Let's pray before we begin.

Father, you have created us for so much more. Reveal to us how to live life in the abundance of your empowering Spirit. May we say with Jesus when our days on this earth are done, "I have glorified you on earth by finishing the work you gave me to do."[1] Amen.

1

Dreaming the Dream

Jacob left Beer-sheba and set out for Haran. He reached a certain place and spent the night there. When the sun had set, he took one of the stones at that place and put it near his head. Then he lay down there. He dreamed and saw a raised staircase, its foundation on earth and its top touching the sky, and God's messengers were ascending and descending on it. Suddenly the LORD was standing on it and saying, "I am the LORD, the God of your father Abraham and the God of Isaac."
(Genesis 28:10-13)

1

Dreaming the Dream

Each year when New Year's Day rolls around, many of us find ourselves setting goals or resolutions for the new year. Lose weight, be on time for work, hit the gym three times a week, reduce yelling at the kids by 25 percent weekly and never yell on Sundays—the list goes on. Those might all be worthwhile goals, but we seriously need to ask ourselves: Am I thinking too small? Am I living the "just get by" plan, or is there a greater God-dream that, if lived to the fullest, could permeate and inform every move I make?

When I tell folks they need to discover God's dreams and visions, many ask what I mean. My wife Carolyn knows. Frequently in this season of our lives I find myself turning to her and saying, "We are living the dream." She knows I don't mean a personal dream or financial dream or even the American dream. I mean something much bigger. It's what Stanford University business professor Jim Collins, author of *Good to Great* and other notable business tomes, calls your BHAG: Big Hairy Audacious Goal.[1] I have had the opportunity to make Jim's acquaintance by speaking at some of the same conferences. I once said to Jim, "I love your idea of the BHAG! In fact I have grabbed it and put my own spin on it. I call it your Big Hairy Audacious God-purpose." What I meant was that God has created each one of us with a particular purpose in his overall creative plan for the universe, and our task in life is to discover that purpose and fulfill it.

Since 1979, Carolyn and I have lived near Dayton, Ohio, hometown of Orville and Wilbur Wright. So, when I think about having a BHAG, the Wright brothers come to mind. Their BHAG was not their day job, which was running a bicycle shop in Dayton, but rather something that had not yet been accomplished: achieving human flight. Fixing bicycles was simply what they did to help fund the dream.

Having a BHAG doesn't have to be limited to the Wright brothers of the world. In Jeremiah 29:11, God says, "I know the plans I have in mind for you." God's plan for you is more than your day job; it's something bigger. It's the purpose God uniquely created for you, the piece you will add to God's mission on earth. In John 20:21, Jesus echoes God's words: "As the Father sent me, so I am sending you."

In *Dare to Dream* you will seek to discern God's purpose for your life, and you will create a life mission statement based on it. You might ask, "How will I recognize my God-purpose when I see it? How will I know it's from God and not from my own self-centered plans and desires?" Here's how: If the purpose is from God, it will always honor God, bless other people, and bring you joy. If it doesn't meet those three criteria, then it isn't a God-purpose, no matter how successful you are in accomplishing it.

Success isn't the key here; significance to the kingdom of God is. In the case of the Wright brothers, their purpose certainly has enhanced the kingdom of God. It's their invention, for example, that enables me to be pastor at Ginghamsburg on a weekend and then teach fellow pastors in Vietnam in the same week. It's what allows Jim Taylor, a longtime Ginghamsburg member and automobile dealership owner, to accomplish his own God-purpose. Jim hosts microbusiness seminars in Cuba, Cambodia, and Jamaica, while running his car dealership at the same time. Jim's God-purpose isn't the car business, although he is very successful at it. It is something so much bigger.

When we dare to dream, we can discern God's dreams for our lives, and following those dreams will help us discover our God-purpose and develop our life mission statement.

Jacob's Dream

As an example of a God-dream, let's look at the story of Jacob in the Old Testament. Jacob eventually became a wealthy, successful businessperson in animal husbandry. In Genesis 28, however, he was on the lam (pun intended). Actually, Jacob had just deceived his elderly father Isaac into giving him the inheritance intended for his older brother Esau. Understandably, Esau was unhappy about his brother's deception, so their parents sent Jacob to stay with extended family for his own safety. We read, starting in Genesis 28:10, that Jacob left Beer-sheba and set out for Haran, about a 750-mile trip. Keep in mind that 750 miles was a significant journey in a time without any kind of motorized transportation.

As the night approached, Jacob stopped at a nondescript place, which the Scripture doesn't even give a name. Jacob took a stone lying nearby and placed it under his head in an attempt to sleep. This would certainly be the ideal setup for a night of restless sleep. Do you ever have restless nights? Note that God often uses restlessness in our lives to get our attention and create change, especially when we find ourselves in a difficult situation. In his sleep, Jacob dreamed that he saw a stairway resting on the earth, its top reaching to heaven, with angels ascending and descending on it. In practical terms that dream doesn't make much sense. We know logically that there are no staircases or ladders connecting earth and heaven. But think about your dreams. How many of those at first don't seem to make sense?

In verses 13 and 14, Jacob saw God standing on the staircase, promising Jacob and his descendants the land on which Jacob was lying. God also promised that Jacob's offspring would become as numerous as the "dust of the earth" and that God would protect Jacob, never leaving him until the promise was fulfilled. Genesis 28:16-17 describes Jacob's reaction:

> When Jacob woke from his sleep, he thought to himself, The LORD is definitely in this place, but I didn't know it. He was terrified and thought, This sacred place is awesome. It's none other than God's house and the entrance to heaven.

As he did for Jacob, God has created for each of us a unique part to play in his creative plan. God is trying to get our attention, so we can live that plan, and God will not leave us until the plan is fulfilled in our lives. That is what I call "living the dream," and it is what I am experiencing in my own life. I am living God's dream for me, and I don't want you to miss yours! Life is too short.

From Self-selected to God-directed

Throughout Scripture, God uses dreams to get people's attention. A shift takes place in Jacob's focus because of this particular dream.

18

Jacob begins to move from his self-selected life path to a God-directed life purpose. We all need to make that shift.

Adults are always asking children, "What do you want to be when you grow up?" At first, we tend to respond with childish answers. When I was a little kid, Roy Rogers was popular, so I wanted to be a cowboy. Then the astronauts rocketed into space, and I wanted to be an astronaut. Eventually, as high school graduation approached, I started thinking about it more carefully: What do I want to do? What do I want to be? There were two choices for many males of my generation: go to college or go to Vietnam. I thought at the time that college would be a better choice.

One of my high school friends was a guy named John. He was two years older than I was and was already attending the University of Cincinnati as a computer science major. I didn't know what computer science was, but I had to apply for something, so I put computer science down. I received a rejection letter from the University of Cincinnati indicating that I didn't have the high school math requirements to get into computer science. The letter named two university programs for which I would be eligible. I don't remember the second one, but the first one was retail management. I had never thought about retail management, but I declared it as my major simply because the program would accept me. How many times do we find ourselves doing things because the opportunity is there and we just kind of fall into it? If that has happened to you, do you ever find yourself asking the question, "Isn't there something more?" None of us wants to miss the "more."

We all go through times of restlessness or difficulty in our lives. Many times that restlessness comes from boredom. People have routines, and routines create ruts. You may notice this trend each Sunday evening on Facebook, where in their statuses people bemoan the return to work and ask how the weekend passed by so quickly. Instead of living in the present and celebrating its gifts, we try to rush through life and get to the next weekend, the next place, the next promotion, or the next spouse. We call Wednesday "hump day" as we start a downhill slide into the longed-for weekend, which is greeted with the cry, "TGIF!"

I am writing this chapter just days after Carolyn and I celebrated our forty-first Christmas as a married couple. Talk about routine! Each year we decorate our house the identical way, placing decorations and memorabilia in the exact same spots. For instance, we have an antique chest of drawers in our entryway where we put our nativity set. As I walked by recently, I picked up a piece of the nativity, looked at it, and set it back down. Later that day I noticed that Carolyn had moved it back three inches because she realized it wasn't where we always put it. We fall into these routines, and routines create ruts.

As a pastor, I see that in worship most of our attendees sit in the same chairs each week. If I run into one of them during my workout at the YMCA, I may not even know the person's name but I will say, "I missed you in worship this week." Since Ginghamsburg is a large church, the person often asks how I knew. It's because I saw the open chair. It's funny to watch how people react on Sunday morning when they find others sitting in "their" seats. We get comfortable and resist change because routines have carved these deep ruts in our lives. That's when God may use dreams to create a restless sleep that will finally get our attention.

Learning from Dreams

So Jacob had this crazy dream with staircases and angels, but it did have a point. Because of the dream, Jacob realized, in that very ordinary place, that God was a powerful presence to which Jacob had previously been oblivious. Jacob then *knew* that God was with him.

Maybe your "crazy" dreams also have a point. I believe our dreams may be the narrowest crossing between heaven and earth, between spiritual and physical, between supernatural and natural. Celtic Christians call these crossings "thin places." A thin place is where you can almost see to the other side; it's where the barrier between natural and supernatural is broken down. The mystics talk about the third eye, with which we see into another dimension and which Hindu women represent by wearing a dot on their foreheads. In Genesis 28, Jacob refers to the entrance to heaven. In early Christian and Jewish traditions, people didn't believe that heaven and earth were far away but existed right next to each other. Dreams provide a bridge between our conscious and subconscious. In the busyness and noise of our daily routines and concerns, our subconscious can only come into play when we are asleep. Through it, we can begin to see to the other side.

Have you ever dreamed about a loved one who has died? I have. My dad died two years ago, but in my dreams about family get-togethers he still shows up. He enters my home with the rest of the family, but he doesn't come right up to me. He sits off to one side. In a recent dream, Dad was sitting away from me in church, eating with a group of people, and he looked at me as I entered the room to teach. This past week, I dreamed that my mom and dad entered my home together. As my mom walked closer, my dad went into another room. But he was still in my house. He exists for me right now, because I can see him in my subconscious. I even dream about my dog, Luka. I know he has died, but in this dream I can pet him. I can feel the knot on his nose and the bump on his head. That is why

I believe Luka will be with me in heaven, the same way John Wesley, the founder of the Wesleyan movement, believed his horse would be in heaven.

When we are awake, we are limited by what we can and cannot do in the physical world. But when our subconscious sees to the other side, those limits disappear. For instance, have you ever been able to fly in your dreams? British author and scholar C. S. Lewis believed that in the next realm we would be able to fly. That is why, in *The Chronicles of Narnia*, Peter, Susan, Edmund, and Lucy are able to fly when they pass into the world of Narnia.[2] If I dream of evil monsters, in my dream I am able to speak the name of Jesus and see the power I have in Christ to banish them. I firmly believe God can speak to us in our dreams. This is why each morning I take time to journal about my dreams and God's message to me as part of my devotional time. As soon as I wake up I begin to forget, and I don't want to lose what God has shared.

Look at Job 33:14: "God speaks in one way, in two ways, but no one perceives it." We often miss God's voice the first time around because of noise, concerns, and routines. But at night God can get our full attention. We go on to read in Job 33:15-18:

> In the dream, a vision of the night,
> when deep sleep falls upon humans,
> during their slumber on a bed,
> then he opens people's ears,
> scares them with warnings,
> to turn them from a deed
> and to smother human pride.
> He keeps one from the pit,
> a life from perishing by the sword.

In the subconscious, dark spirits lurk that we aren't always aware of in our waking life. In my dreams, sometimes I am warned of temptations that could harm or destroy me, the people I love, and those who look to me for leadership. Here's an example from a dream I had last summer, which I immediately journaled about the next morning.

In my dream I am driving through a low-income neighborhood in the West College Hill district of Cincinnati, an economically challenged area where early in my ministry I worked as a pastor with many young people. In fact, when I was nineteen, it was two churches in this community, one Baptist and one A.M.E., which first let me preach. As I drive down the street in my dream, a toddler girl is sitting and playing in the middle of the road. I swerve left and then right to miss her. With heart racing, I look in my rearview mirror. I didn't hit her, but she is still sitting there.

Some dreams are so real, so vivid. When I woke up, my heart was pounding, and my body was covered in a cold sweat. Here is what I believe God was saying to me through that dream.

At the time, I had been worrying about the work of Ginghamsburg Church in Darfur, Sudan. We had served in Darfur since 2005, investing over $6 million dollars in sustainable humanitarian projects including agriculture, safe water, and child development and protection. I had been fretting over the upcoming Christmas Miracle Offering to fund the project for the next year. It would be our ninth time to call the Ginghamsburg family to sacrificial giving at Christmas, and I was concerned about the "compassion fatigue" that might have settled in. In the early days, as our hearts were touched by the Darfuris' plight and the first genocide of the twenty-first century, it was easier to feel good about sacrifice and making a significant difference in people's lives. But sometimes we can get tired, just worn out, with compassion exhausted. I feared our people had reached that point. I wondered if we should be doing something else.

What God said to me so vividly in that dream was, "You might not have hit that little girl in the street, but it's not enough just to pass her by. You have got to go back and get that kid out of the street so no one else hits her." In essence, the Lord said to me, "Mike, this ten years of feeling good about working in one place is not what it means to be a follower of Jesus; you need to keep taking care of the children, whether they are sitting in the street in Dayton, Ohio, or struggling to survive in Darfur, Sudan." God reminded me I had signed up for life! God used that dream to get my attention.

Waking Visions

Of course, God also can speak to us through visions when we are awake. Let's take a look at Acts 9:10-12:

> In Damascus there was a certain disciple named Ananias. The Lord spoke to him in a vision, "Ananias!" He answered, "Yes, Lord." The Lord instructed him, "Go to Judas' house on Straight Street and ask for a man from Tarsus named Saul. He is praying. In a vision he has seen a man named Ananias enter and put his hands on him to restore his sight."

It's interesting how specific this vision is. Have you ever been sitting in your house watching TV or totally engrossed in what you were doing, only to have a person's name pop into your head? There's a chance that such thoughts may come from God. If the thought is good or appropriate, then I believe it's from God. I know that whenever it happens to me, no matter how involved I am in what I am doing, I need to get up and call that person or take the action that God has brought to mind. These types of experiences are visions. It's the Holy Spirit moving, and there is nothing more important for me to do at that moment than respond. God speaks through dreams when we are asleep, and God speaks through visions when we are awake.

As I write this book, Ginghamsburg Church is celebrating its 150th anniversary. In 1863, a circuit rider named B. W. Day preached in Vandalia, just south of our current location, at a two-week revival meeting. A circuit rider was a preacher who rode around the country preaching and would stay at each place for a few weeks. Then the believers, if they were so moved, would start a faith community. When B. W. finished the revival in Vandalia, he had a vision to visit a tiny burg of a place called Ginghamsburg and preach a revival. But it didn't really make sense. Vandalia was a thriving little town, but Ginghamsburg was only twenty-two houses with a post office and a community center. The town didn't even have a church. But B. W. was convinced God had spoken and declared that a movement would be birthed out of Ginghamsburg that would influence the world. B. W. was obedient to the vision. He came to Ginghamsburg and preached his heart out for two weeks, resulting in eighteen conversions. Now, that isn't much to show for preaching your heart out. But ten of those eighteen new believers decided to create this faith community called Ginghamsburg Church, believing B. W. Day's vision that Ginghamsburg would grow into a movement that would influence the world. And, thanks to generations of faithful Christians who followed, it did.

As B. W. Day knew, God speaks to us in visions while we are awake. For that to happen, of course, we must make space in our lives to be present to God's presence. We must make time for what the ancients called contemplation. God is here, but I have to make myself aware; I must become intimate with the Third Person of the Trinity, the

Holy Spirit. We study about God the Father: God is love. We study about God the Son: Jesus is the redeemer who revealed the Father to us. We know the least about the Holy Spirit, and yet it is in this form that God communicates our purpose to each of us. Many of us complain that we never hear a word from God, much less receive a vision, but we also don't do anything about developing the relationship. We will never hear or sense the work of the Spirit if we don't invest time each day in praying, examining God's word, and listening for God's voice.

Jesus said in John 14:16-19*a*, "I will ask the Father, and he will send another Companion, who will be with you forever. This Companion is the Spirit of Truth. . . . I won't leave you as orphans. I will come to you. Soon the world will no longer see me, but you will see me." That is what the Holy Spirit allows us to do while we're awake: to see the Spirit in the thin places, serving as the third eye into that which is otherwise unseen. The Spirit, Jesus taught, will lead us into all truth, guiding us in what is to come.

A Life Mission Statement

Before you move on to the next chapter, take some time in prayer and discernment to work through the questions that follow. Your responses to these and other questions at the end of Chapters 1–5 will serve as the foundation for your life mission statement. Then, at the end of Chapter 6, you will build your life mission statement.

Let me help to get you started on the questions below. I've asked you to identify three people you admire and then answer questions about them. As an example, I will name one of the three people I listed: Bono, lead singer for the rock group U2.

Bono's BHAG is not his day job, which is rock music. He loves his music, I'm sure, and it has blessed his family. However, his passion is eliminating extreme poverty, especially in Africa. He has focused on many of the same needs in the greater African continent that Ginghamsburg Church has dealt with in Darfur.

Bono spoke at my son's college graduation from the University of Pennsylvania, and he was the best graduation speaker I've ever heard. He came walking out in his robe with his boots on and hair flowing, and all those Ivy League grads rose to their feet to cheer him. Bono said, "But no, I never went to college; I've slept in some strange places, but the library wasn't one of them." Then he shared his BHAG about eliminating extreme poverty in Africa. To paraphrase the end of his speech he basically was challenging them, "That's what I'm doing with my life; what are you Ivy League graduates going to do with yours?"[3]

The quality I admire in Bono is that he demonstrates life is not about success but about service. Life is not about chasing the money; it's about chasing the mission. And when you chase the mission, God will go with you.

My goal in the pages ahead is to awaken the God-dream in you and unlock the gift of what it means to live that dream—a dream that honors God, blesses others, and brings you joy. Now, let's get to work on those questions.

Building Your Life Mission Statement

Part 1

Identify three people you admire, and ask the following questions about them:

- What are the greatest qualities that you think these people exemplify?

- What steps have these people taken to nurture these qualities?

- Why are these qualities important to you? How would your life be different if you lived more effectively into these qualities?

Notes

2

Discovering Your Birthright

He gave some apostles, some prophets, some evangelists, and some pastors and teachers. His purpose was to equip God's people for the work of serving and building up the body of Christ until we all reach the unity of faith and knowledge of God's Son. God's goal is for us to become mature adults—to be fully grown, measured by the standard of the fullness of Christ.

(Ephesians 4:11-13)

2

Discovering Your Birthright

When God puts a dream inside you, it's not just for you. A God-dream will honor God and bless other people in tangible ways. It's your birthright. Let's explore how we discover our birthright as we lean fully into the purpose for which we've been created.

God has created every one of us for a particular purpose. For the majority of us, that purpose will not be our day job. I used Bono as an example in the last chapter. Bono describes his first day job as a venture capitalist and second day job as a musician.[1] However, his BHAG is to eliminate extreme poverty. His God-dream is much bigger than his day job.

Rick Warren, of Saddleback Church in California, wrote *The Purpose Driven Life*[2]—a great book to read, by the way, as you develop your life mission statement. *The Purpose Driven Life* has been translated into fifty-six languages and has sold over thirty million copies worldwide. Rick Warren's day job is pastor, and he's a great one. But his BHAG is to eliminate AIDS in the world. He has contributed so much to the fight against AIDS in Rwanda that the president of Rwanda has made him an official member of his cabinet. Now that's a cool BHAG!

What's at the Top of Your Ladder?

We talked in Chapter 1 about Jacob and his dream. In the dream he saw a staircase, or ladder, with angels going up and down. Most important, though, was what Jacob saw at the top of the ladder. It was God. Stop for a moment and ask yourself what's at the top of your ladder. Your life dreams will be limited by the ceiling of your life pictures. What limitations are your life pictures placing on you?

When Jacob saw God at the top of the ladder, God revealed not Jacob's day job but his BHAG—the life mission for which Jacob was created, in the form of God's promise of countless offspring and enduring protection. Let's continue Jacob's story:

> After Jacob got up early in the morning, he took the stone that he had put near his head, set it up as a sacred pillar, and poured oil on the top of it. He named that sacred place Bethel. (Genesis 28:18-19)

At that point, God had really gotten Jacob's attention, and Jacob was beginning to recognize his God-dream. Jacob then made a promise to God:

> "If God is with me and protects me on this trip I'm taking, and gives me bread to eat and clothes to wear, and I return safely to my father's household, then the LORD will be my God. This stone that I've set up as a sacred pillar will be God's house, and of everything you give me I will give a tenth back to you." (vv. 20-22)

I love God's patience. Did you notice all "ifs" and "buts" implied in Jacob's response? The Lord would be his God *if* Jacob was protected, got food to eat and clothes to wear, made it back to his father in one piece, and on and on. There were so many conditions to his commitment! To move forward, Jacob would have to lose his "big buts," which we will talk about in Chapter 4. For now, though, Jacob was at least beginning to understand God had a dream for him that was greater than being a successful herder.

In fact, God had a change-the-world purpose not just for Jacob's life but for all our lives before we were born. You might think, "Who, me?" But the Book of Jeremiah proclaims, "I know the plans I have in mind for you, declares the LORD" (Jeremiah 29:11). And Jesus said, "I assure you that whoever believes in me will do the works that I do. They will do even greater works than these" (John 14:12).

Don't let the scope of your dreams be limited by the ceiling of your life pictures! Many of us initially respond as Moses did when God told him (paraphrase of Exodus 3:7-11), "I hear the cries of my children who are in bondage in Egypt, and I'm going to send you." Moses responded, "Who am I that you would send me? There are far more gifted people. There are better people. There are people who don't struggle in their faith the way I do, Lord. There are people who demonstrate a higher character level than I do, Lord." Sound familiar?

But here's the thing: God doesn't make mistakes. When you were created, God knew the plan for your life. God won't back out of it. God won't quit. Jacob is a perfect example. Jacob's very name, according to Esau in Genesis 27:36, meant what most of us today would call identity theft. He had taken the birthright and blessing of his brother and was on the run, fearing retribution. And yet God had a great dream for Jacob's life.

Discovering Your Identity

I was fortunate as a young pastor. I became part of a group of pastors, all in our thirties, who were identified as anointed and "called" young leaders by some wealthy and successful Christian business people. Those business people invited us to a retreat center in Colorado, where they explained how they wanted to invest in our lives. They saw us as having big potential for taking the gospel out into the world. But they also knew that we were untrained in terms of business process, management, and systems. They announced they were going to send us to some of the best businesses in the country so that we might learn how to do more with the gifts that God had given us.

One of the companies where we met with top executives was Southwest Airlines, which has remained about the only consistently profitable airline in the country. Another company we visited was DreamWorks Animation, where we served as consultants with Jeffrey Katzenberg on the animated movie *Prince of Egypt* (1998). Then we went to Harley-Davidson, the number-one motorcycle company in the world. (Harley-Davidson even sells more motorcycles in Asia than its Asian competitor, Honda.)

I found our time with Harley-Davidson particularly interesting, as I learned from one of their top executives that Harley-Davidson isn't really selling motorcycles; it is selling identity. The executive explained that the profit margins on motorcycles are pretty slim. What Harley really makes a bundle on are clothing, drinking glasses, and pool tables. He then taught us the theology of tattoos. He said to make sure to notice people's tattoos because people put on their bodies the things that are most important to them—in other words, what's at the top of their ladder. He said, "You'll notice that no one in the world goes around with a Honda tattoo."

All of a sudden, I began to see the genius of Harley in selling identity. I looked at people's tattoos at the gym when I worked out. What were their identities? I saw Ohio State tattoos. I saw Cleveland Browns and Cincinnati Bengals tattoos. I even saw Woody Woodpecker.

Later, I bought a Harley motorcycle. I purchased some Harley clothing, too, but it's not my identity. Who or what is at the top of your ladder? If it's anything other than God, you're limiting your life dreams.

Have you seen the movie called *Catch Me If You Can* (DreamWorks, 2002)? Leonardo DiCaprio plays a real-life con artist named Frank Abagnale, who during his career took on many different identities. He traveled around the world writing bad checks to support a lifestyle he didn't earn. For instance, he presented himself as an airline pilot. Fortunately, he didn't fly the plane; he just wore the uniform so that he could ride for free in the jump seat. He also posed as a college professor and as a lawyer. Perhaps his scariest gig was when he took on the false identity of a doctor! Tom Hanks plays the persevering FBI agent who eventually tracked Abagnale down for stealing other people's identities. Eventually, Abagnale went to prison.

God often gets our attention in our brokenness, and that's when we discover our true birthright. Frank Abagnale discovered his while in prison. He didn't have to steal the identity of an airplane pilot, doctor, or professor. Today he is CEO of a security company he founded, and his number-one customer is the FBI. Abagnale helps the FBI track down identity theft, ultimately making our identities more secure. That's his true birthright.

Identity and birthright are not the same. All of us share the same identity: we are children of God, living under the kingship of Jesus

Christ. Birthright, on the other hand, is the individual purpose that God has for you. It's why God created you, and it's about your mission on Planet Earth—a mission that will honor God, bless people, and bring you joy.

Charles Colson is another example of finding birthright in a time of brokenness. Colson was special counselor to Richard Nixon during the Watergate scandal. Of all those convicted for Watergate-related crimes, he spent the longest time in prison. He was not a person of faith and was often described as one of the meanest people in the Nixon administration. So, what happened to Colson in prison? He found Jesus. I was a young Jesus freak in seminary at the time, and boy, did his story go viral, even without the Internet! Colson later said "being sent to prison—was the beginning of God's greatest use of my life."[3] That use wasn't about his day job as an attorney or the president's "hatchet man." What emerged from the scandal was his God-purpose. Charles Colson created a ministry called Prison Fellowship that has since changed the lives of countless prisoners around the world.

A Vision of Sudan

My day job is pastor. Nine years ago, God came to me in a vision while I was awake. He said, "The first genocide of the twenty-first century is happening in Sudan, and I want you to do something about it." My reaction? Hey, I don't have any power—I'm a pastor! Isn't this something the government should tackle? But visions happen when we pay attention to what God is doing and saying.

Looking back on it, the seed had been planted five years earlier. I had arrived home from Ginghamsburg one Sunday afternoon and opened up the newspaper. On the left side of the page was an article about famine and devastation from the twenty-year civil war in the Sudan. It included a heartbreaking photo of an emaciated child. Now, I struggle with materialism, so my gaze was drawn to the right of the page, where a brand-new BMW 7 Series sedan was offered for lease. The lease for that BMW was $649 per month, with $5,000 down and a limit of 10,000 miles per year. I knew all about its luxury features, including the sixteen-speaker Bose sound system. Eventually I pulled my eyes away, remembered the child's photo, and read about the masses starving in Sudan because of drought and war. At the time, it troubled me that I knew so much more about the sedan than the Sudan.

Five years later, God spoke, challenging me to help in Sudan. I shouldn't have been surprised. In Genesis, God said, "I am with you now, I will protect you everywhere you go, and I will bring you back to this land. I will not leave you until I have done everything that I have promised you" (Genesis 28:15). God would ensure that this change-the-world purpose happened through my life.

Since that day, Ginghamsburg Church has invested over $6 million and affected the lives of tens of thousands of individuals in Darfur. Our investment has attracted an additional $17 million from others. I've been able to go around the world—South Korea, Germany, Denmark, Northern Ireland, and college campuses across America—telling people about the plight of Sudan.

Here's the key: the only way we can discover our birthright is through an intimate relationship with God the Holy Spirit. If all we study is God the Father and God the Son, we will know *about* God, but we won't *know* God in an intimate relationship through the Holy Spirit. This is why I think many Christians may stand before the Father on Judgment Day unable to say, "I've finished the work for which you sent me." Instead they will be saying, "I didn't even know what the work was!

The Bible provides general revelation for all of us. But it's through the Holy Spirit that you will find God's purpose for you specifically. Some may proclaim after reading this that I am downplaying the Bible. I am not. It is God's precious word for all of us. But the specific revelation from God about his unique plan for you comes through the Holy Spirit.

Personally, I can't afford to overlook the Spirit. I am sixty-two years old. I am almost dead! I don't have time to mess around. I have got to finish the work God has sent me to do.

Hearing the Holy Spirit

What does Scripture say about hearing the voice of the Holy Spirit? Let's start with Paul's first letter to the Corinthians.

God has prepared things for those who love him that no eye has seen, or ear has heard, or that haven't crossed the mind of any human being. God has revealed these things to us through the Spirit. The Spirit searches everything, including the depths of God. (1 Corinthians 2:9-10)

That is huge! What you can't learn in any university, what you can't even think of or imagine in your finite mind—all of this God reveals to us by the Holy Spirit. Try to imagine this infinite God, a God who keeps expanding and creating the universe, a God whose thoughts are infinite. Well, the Spirit knows God's intimate thoughts because the Spirit is God, and you can know the Spirit. Paul continues:

Who knows a person's depths except their own spirit that lives in them? In the same way, no one has known the depths of God except God's Spirit. We haven't received the world's spirit but God's Spirit so that we can know the things given to us by God. . . . Spiritual people comprehend everything. (2:11-12, 15)

God comes into our lives through the Spirit serving as the ladder that connects us and leads us in all things to come. We know God through an intimate relationship with the Holy Spirit.

We can see the Holy Spirit at work in the story of Paul. In Galatians 1:1, Paul describes himself as "an apostle who is not sent from human authority or commissioned through human agency, but sent through Jesus Christ and God the Father who raised him from the dead." How did Paul know that he was an apostle and that he wasn't commissioned through human hands? He didn't read it in the Bible or learn it in seminary. He tells us the answer in Galatians 2:1-2: "Then after fourteen years I went up to Jerusalem again with Barnabas, and I took Titus along also. I went there because of a revelation, and I laid out the gospel that I preach to the Gentiles for them."

Where did Paul receive his revelation, his BHAG? When did it happen? Think about it: Paul never met Jesus in the physical body. Paul understood his identity, birthright, and BHAG; he knew what God the Father and God the Son were doing, all because of his relationship with the Holy Spirit.

My Life Mission Statement

Do you know what your birthright is? Ephesians 4:11 indicates that God has equipped people to be apostles, prophets, evangelists, pastors, and teachers. How many people reading this book have those life purposes and don't even know it? Who is at the top of your ladder?

What Jacob discovered when he saw God at the top of the ladder in his dream was a revelation of God's presence. Jacob discovered his true birthright. It wasn't being a con man who steals other people's identities. Rather, God created him for a unique mission on earth. The mission, which had a lot of "ifs" and "buts," would need some clarifying. But God kept working on him. In Genesis 32, God changed his name from Jacob, con man, to Israel, which means one who struggles with God.

Note what Jacob did in Genesis 28:18 after his dream: "After Jacob got up early in the morning, he took the stone that he had put near his head, set it up as a sacred pillar, and poured oil on the top of it." In the Old Testament, when people had visions of God, they would sometimes take a stone and, to commemorate the experience, put it in a nearby place where they regularly traveled or walked. The expression "You can write it in stone" comes from this concept of a memorial stone.

Today, for you and me, we might consider placing an object that acts as a memorial stone in our office, factory, or home as a reminder of the God-mission in our lives. When I walk out of my office at night, I might be tired, cranky, and hungry. But then I see my memorial stone. It reminds me of the work for which I was sent. It keeps me from getting so distracted by the daily grind of my day job that I'm not finishing my God-purpose.

My life mission statement serves as my memorial stone. It is different from my goals, which may change with the season or circumstance. It describes my God-purpose and is what I will use in saying to the Father on Judgment Day, "I have finished the work that you called me to do."

I keep my memorial stone in the front of my daily journal. My mission statement hasn't changed in over forty years; I just keep copying it into the new journal each time I fill one up. Two pages after the mission statement, I write the strategic steps I plan to follow during the current year to accomplish my life mission. I'll share my life mission statement with you; but remember, you'll want to write your own.

First, at the top of the journal page I always write:

Life Mission: "I glorified you on earth by finishing the work that you gave me to do." (John 17:4 NRSV)

Then I write my life mission statement, which has three parts.

1. To raise a family that will influence our future generations for Jesus.

From the time my kids were little, they were in Sunday school. We studied the Bible with them at home. They were in life groups as teenagers. If they didn't feel like attending youth group, they still had to go. Even on our vacations, when it might be the last thing we wanted to do, we went to church. We went because we were teaching our children what was supposed to be at the top of the ladder.

In my son's sophomore year of high school he was playing three sports, so I said, "You've got to go on a mission trip during football, basketball, or baseball season. You pick." So he chose to take a week off during basketball season to go on a mission trip. As a result, his coach benched him for three games when he got back. What was I teaching my son? Sports aren't going to be at the top of your ladder.

2. To raise up a church that will demonstrate the kingdom of God on earth.

When I wrote the second part of my mission statement, I didn't mean that I wanted people simply to attend church. A church's measure of greatness isn't the number of behinds in pews; it's how many are actively serving the mission of Jesus Christ.

3. To equip church leaders who will reach future generations.

Each year I take on tasks to advance this third part of my mission statement. This year I've taught pastors in Vietnam and at a pastors' conference in Copenhagen, and I've spoken at various conferences around the U.S. I want to make sure that I order my priorities around all three parts of my life mission.

Three Questions

I have had this same life mission since I was nineteen. When I was a Jesus freak at the University of Cincinnati, I was blessed by having a great mentor who insisted on the importance of a life mission statement. He recommended that I find it by asking three questions. The first question was, "Where do you see the greatest need around you in your neighborhood, your community, or your world?" For me, I saw the greatest need in the local church. My church had bored me when I was a kid, and I saw it as completely irrelevant to the needs of the community where it was located. In fact I was surrounded by churches in every neighborhood that seemed impotent or dead. I thought to myself: "Can you imagine what would happen if the local church got it? We could change the world one neighborhood at a time!"

The second question was, "How can you meet that need?" I knew that for me to help meet the needs in the local church, I would have to be on the inside, putting my hand on the rudder. The church wouldn't magically change; I would need to help lead that change. That scared me. The last thing I wanted to be was a pastor! The most positive picture of a pastor that I had at the time was Mr. Rogers, a Presbyterian minister with a BHAG to give kids everywhere healthy images about themselves and their lives via television. I'll bet that when he met God at the pearly gates, Mr. Rogers said with integrity, "I finished the work you sent me to do." Starting with that picture, I began coming to terms with the role of pastor and what it might mean in my life.

The final question was: "What gifts do you bring to further that mission?" Please hear me: I didn't know what gifts I had. However, I came to realize that you don't discover your gifts and then serve; your gifts emerge out of your service. So I jumped in and began working with the teens in my church, even though I was still a teenager myself. I discovered that when I taught, young people seemed to like it. They would say things such as, "Mike, when you teach the Bible, you break it down to the least complicated denominator. I get it!" What they were responding to was not my ability to do counseling, which is a gift that many pastors have but clearly I do not. Instead, I was being called to further this mission by using my gift of teaching.

Those three questions were a tremendous help to me in discerning my God-purpose and developing my life mission statement. I feel confident that they can help you, too.

There's one important addendum to the three questions, and you'll find it in the story of Jacob. In Genesis 28:22, Jacob promised, "This stone that I've set up as a sacred pillar will be God's house, and of everything you give me I will give a tenth back to you."

My life mission statement reminds me of the work God has sent me to do, and part of accomplishing that work is giving back to God a tenth of everything that comes into my hand. The practical commitment of the ten-percent tithe is absolutely essential to demonstrate my submission to the kingship of Jesus Christ.[4]

God has created you for a change-the-world purpose. You need to uncover it. The last thing you want to do is stand before the Father on Judgment Day and say, "I didn't even know what my life purpose was." Before we go on, let me pray for us, and then we will get to work on those questions.

Father God, I am so thankful that in spite of our failures and distractions, you don't quit on us. You continually call us to live the great purpose for which you created us. Lord, empower us as we risk daring to dream your dream. In Jesus' name. Amen.

Building Your Life
Mission Statement

Part 2

In preparing to create your life mission statement, answer these three questions:

- Where do you see the greatest need around you in your neighborhood, your community, or your world?

- How can you meet that need?

- What gifts do you bring to further that mission?

Notes

3

Your Burning Bush

When the Lord saw that he was coming to look, God called to him out of the bush, "Moses, Moses!"

Moses said, "I'm here."

Then the Lord said, "Don't come any closer! Take off your sandals, because you are standing on holy ground." He continued, "I am the God of your father, Abraham's God, Isaac's God, and Jacob's God." Moses hid his face because he was afraid to look at God.

(Exodus 3:4-6)

3

Your Burning Bush

A rally was held on April 3, 1968, at Bishop Charles Mason Temple in Memphis, Tennessee, in support of the Memphis Sanitation Strike. More than 1,300 African American sanitation workers had walked off the job the previous February to protest their poor treatment and dangerous working conditions. Martin Luther King Jr., not feeling well and exhausted from his travels, wasn't expected to show up. But he did, delivering what came to be known as his "I've Been to the Mountaintop" speech. Here is an excerpt:

> We've got some difficult days ahead. But it really doesn't matter with me now, because I've been to the mountaintop. And I don't mind. Like anybody, I would like to live a long life—longevity has its place. But I'm not concerned about that now. I just want to do God's will. And He's allowed me to go up to the mountain. And I've looked over, and I've seen the Promised Land. I may not get there with you. But I want you to know tonight, that we, as a people, will get to the Promised Land. And so I'm happy,

tonight; I'm not worried about anything. I'm not fearing any man. Mine eyes have seen the glory of the coming of the Lord.[1]

It was the last speech Dr. King would give; he was assassinated the next day. His words always remind me of what he knew so well. There is something much more important than living a long life, and that is doing the will of God, however long we live. Dr. King clearly had recognized God's dream for himself, and he worked his entire life to achieve it.

Like Dr. King, you have been created to be a part of God's redemptive mission in the world. You weren't sent to Planet Earth just to eat food and make a living; you were meant to experience and carry out God's dream. Part of identifying that dream is to encounter a burning bush.

Let's look at how it happened for Moses in Exodus 3. By that time, Moses had been living in the land of Midian for forty years, taking care of his father-in-law's flock. One day he was tending the sheep near Horeb, known as the "mountain of God," when he spotted a bush that appeared to be on fire yet wasn't being burned up. Not surprisingly, that got Moses' attention, so he stopped to check it out.

The Lord spoke to him from within the bush, directing Moses to remove his sandals because he was standing on holy ground. Frightened, Moses hid his face. But God went on: "The cry of the Israelites has now come to me; I have also seen how the Egyptians oppress them. So come, I will send you to Pharaoh to bring my people, the Israelites, out of Egypt" (Exodus 3:9-10 NRSV).

Moses encountered a burning bush, and you will too if you look for it. The ultimate hunger, thirst, and passion that all of us feel is to find the reason we were created. Even though we can't always name that hunger, and we often try to satisfy it with other things, all of us want to know our life purpose.

We can learn a lot about discovering our life purpose by studying the story of Moses. It reveals three life stages that all of us go through in the process of finding our purpose. For Moses, those life stages just happened to come in three segments of forty years each.

Stage 1: Empire Building

The first forty years of Moses' life demonstrated what I call self-ascension, or empire building. Moses was born a Hebrew slave, but Pharaoh had issued a mandate at the time of his birth to kill all Hebrew babies. Pharaoh feared the Hebrews were becoming too populous and worried about what would happen if the slaves ever decided to revolt. So Moses' mother took a basket, covered it with pitch, and hid the handcrafted lifeboat in the reeds of the Nile River with Moses inside. Pharaoh's daughter found the baby along the shore and adopted him as her own. From an early age Moses was consumed by his role as prince of Egypt and what it would mean for him to lead the powerful empire. Using the metaphor of ladder climbing, we can say that during this first stage on the bottom rungs, Moses was completely absorbed by his own wants and needs.

All of us go through this stage. We attend school to educate ourselves for the future, then go off to college or start a career. Relationships happen. Some of us marry and have a family. At this stage we aren't usually asking, "God, what is your will for my life?" We are more focused on getting God to bless our endeavors, praying, "Oh God, if I could only get a date with that girl" or "If I could only get that promotion, God." These are "God bless me" prayers. Everything is about ladder climbing. In this stage, if we ask ourselves who is at the top of our ladder and answer truthfully, it usually isn't God, even if we claim to believe in God. We aren't really looking for

God's will, but instead we are trying to make God's will fit into and support our own.

Jesus gave a great example of Stage 1 living in Luke 14:16-24. In this parable he told of a man, representing God, who threw an incredible party. In the story, people had all kinds of excuses for not showing up: "I need to check on my farm." "Just bought some oxen that need my attention." "I am recently married and tied up with the wife." All the excuses had to do with people fulfilling their own needs. We are invited to participate in the abundant life of God's mission on earth, and many of us turn down the invitation. We rationalize, focusing on our own needs and telling ourselves that eventually we will find time to think about God's needs. Eventually.

For most of us, the three forces driving Stage 1 are the same three forces Jesus confronted during his forty days in the wilderness: appetite, approval, and ambition.

Appetite

Remember when a hungry Jesus was tempted by Satan to turn stones into bread? Most of us have experienced this first driving force, which is based on *I want*: "I want that job." "I want that car." "I want that house." We are focused on accumulating all the right stuff, which we think will fill our deep desire to find purpose in life. And, of course, it doesn't. Appetite, in fact, helped create the economic collapse of 2008. Before the economic bubble burst, people were driven by their appetites to live a lifestyle greater than they could afford. In 2005, Americans were spending $1.22 for every dollar they earned. We turned that around briefly after the recession started and began saving more than we spent, but within a few years we had slipped back into bad financial habits.

Approval

The next driving force is approval, which often begins with peer pressure. When I started high school, one of the things I decided never to do was drink alcohol. Then one of my good buddies said, "Mike, try this beer. Everybody who's anybody is drinking beer." I tasted my first beer in ninth grade. I said to my friend, "Man, this is terrible! Give me my Mountain Dew." He said, "Oh no, you have to develop a taste for it." (That should have been a hint right there.) For many people this quest for approval happened in college, where we did things we had sworn we would never do, such as pulling crazy stunts to impress our friends or striving to get accepted into a fraternity or sorority. In the case of Jesus, Satan took him to the highest place, the pinnacle of the Temple in Jerusalem, and told him to jump off. Satan said, "You are the Son of God. God is not going to let you hurt yourself, and everyone will cheer you on!" Most of us are driven in some way by this need for recognition or celebrity. We want approval.

Ambition

The third driving force is ambition, which we've talked about in the metaphor of ladder climbing. Satan took Jesus and showed him all the kingdoms of the world, saying, "You came for the world, right? Wasn't that your mission, Jesus? I will give it to you, and you won't have to go through all that messy and painful God-stuff like the cross." This is where the "God bless me" prayers come in. As Christians, we read in the Bible that we are to love and serve God with all our heart, soul, mind, and strength (Mark 12:30 NRSV). But we rationalize it away, saying, "I'll do that eventually, but right now I'm busy raising kids, working, paying the bills, and mowing the grass. I'll get around to it eventually."

Stage 2: Disillusionment

Stage two is disillusionment, which usually is initiated by crisis. For Moses, the crisis happened at age forty, and it had to do with anger-management issues. Moses had been given a name that was Egyptian, not Hebrew, but he still had a distant memory of his Hebrew ancestry. One day when he was out supervising slaves, he saw the slave masters beating Hebrew slaves. Moses became so furious at one slave master that he killed him. Now, even if you were prince of Egypt you didn't kill an Egyptian citizen. Moses had to flee, and he became a sheepherder in the land of Midian, where he lived and worked for the next forty years of his life. No doubt, being a sheepherder was tremendously different from being the prince of Egypt. A change like that will get your attention.

The disillusionment that Moses experienced was what today we might call a midlife crisis. Perhaps at first you thought marriage would be the best thing ever, that your spouse would satisfy your deep hunger and thirst for fulfillment and significance. Then you reached the top of that particular ladder only to discover that the void was still there. That's when some of us start extramarital affairs, get divorced, or simply begin to live passionless, parallel existences. My wife Carolyn is the best woman in the whole world; no other woman could ever measure up. However, even Carolyn can't satisfy the hunger, thirst, and passion that I feel to fulfill God's purpose for my life.

For others of us, disillusionment may come through the loss of a job. We've worked hard and done everything right, and suddenly we are laid off, asking, "Why has this happened to me?" Or disillusionment may come through sickness or loss. Life presents so many tragedies, and as a pastor I am exposed to a lot of them. Just a few days ago, Ginghamsburg Church conducted a funeral for a promising young woman from a nearby university who died in a house fire. Bad stuff happens to innocent people!

When we hit Stage 2, the prayer is no longer "God bless me." Instead, the prayer is "God save me." It's at this point when we are most receptive to a burning bush, allowing us to move into Stage 3.

Stage 3: A Fire That Won't Burn Out

Let's return to the moment when Moses saw the burning bush.

> There the angel of the LORD appeared to him in a flame of fire out of a bush; he looked, and the bush was blazing, yet it was not consumed. Then Moses said, 'I must turn aside and look at this great sight, and see why the bush is not burned up.'" (Exodus 3:2-3 NRSV)

Isn't it interesting that the bush wasn't burned up by the fire? When you encounter your burning bush—a defining event that leads you to your life purpose—it creates a fire in you that will not burn out.

When I was a teenager, I was part of a rock band that was busted for drug possession. We thought we were climbing the rock 'n' roll ladder to fame and fortune. Before that incident happened, we had been scheduled to open for the rock band Steppenwolf at the Cincinnati Gardens. When we were busted for drugs, I had my "Jesus, save me!" moment, and God called me to ministry.

I was eighteen years old and told my parents about my new calling. My dad was understandably skeptical. "This is just another trip you're on," he said. "It will last six months, like everything else you've done, and then it will be gone." I can understand why he said that;

I had given him good reason in the past to believe it. But it was my burning bush, and it didn't flame out. A true God-purpose will not burn you out or burn you up.

Notice that when Moses saw the burning bush he said, "I must turn aside." It's true for all of us. We must turn away from dull daily routines and lackluster lives—from the "same old, same old" that we have been doing year after year. When we change our priorities and replace what's at the top of our ladder, we are in Stage 3. We understand then, as Moses did, that no matter where our feet happen to be planted, we are standing on holy ground. We realize, *I am not self-created. It is not about me.* It is just as Jesus taught: "Those who find their lives will lose them, and those who lose their lives because of me will find them" (Matthew 10:39). Or as John the Baptist said, "He must increase and I must decrease" (John 3:30).

Burning Bush Moments

A burning bush moment is when you hear God speak in a personal way so that you can know your purpose. When Moses stood before the burning bush, he saw an angel of the Lord. In Hebrew, the word we translate as *angel* means "messenger." An angel can be a celestial messenger, such as when the angel Gabriel told Mary she would be pregnant with Jesus. God can also speak through a human messenger, as in Genesis 18, when three men showed up at the door of Abraham's tent and announced that his elderly wife Sarah would become pregnant. Sarah, who was well past her childbearing years, broke into bellyaching, uncontrollable laughter. A year later, they had a son.

When I look back, I see that God has sent many messengers into my life—people who asked me, even as a young child, if I had ever thought about being a minister. How has God spoken to you over your lifetime, and whom has God used to do so?

I am often asked when I teach about life dreams how to hear God's voice. As I mentioned, I was honored to serve as one of the theologians who consulted on the DreamWorks motion picture called *Prince of Egypt*. Jeffrey Katzenberg, who headed the project, was struggling theologically with how to represent the voice that spoke to Moses from the bush. One idea was to use people from all over the world with different accents speaking the words in chorus together. However, our group of theologians pointed out that we most often hear God as a quiet inner voice—not as an external or audible voice. As a result, in the final version of the burning bush scene we hear actor Val Kilmer, who was the voice of Moses, reading the parts of both Moses and God. See if you think it works when you watch the movie. We most often hear God in this inner voice; that is the Holy Spirit speaking to us. Remember, Jesus said in John 16 that he was going away but would send to us a Companion (v. 7) who would guide us in all truth and reveal what is to come.

Notice that Moses' burning bush experience and the mission it revealed were deeply tied to his life experiences. As a baby, Moses had been a target of genocide. Growing up, he had witnessed beatings and ill treatment of Hebrews. As an adult, he saw first-hand the oppression and injustices that the Egyptians visited upon slaves. All these experiences came together at Moses' burning bush.

As you think about your own burning bush, keep in mind that it may be tied to some of your deepest and most painful life experiences. These difficulties may very well be clues to the places or opportunities where God has called you to act.

Martin Luther King Jr. talked about a burning bush in his life. When he was little, his father, a pastor at Ebenezer Baptist Church in downtown Atlanta, took young Martin into a store to buy shoes. When they sat down in the front of the store, a salesperson came over and said, "I'll be happy to wait on you if you'll just move to those seats in the rear."

"We'll either buy shoes sitting here," Martin's father replied, "or we won't buy shoes at all." He took young Martin's hand, and they walked out of the store together.[2] That early experience helped pave the way for Dr. King's ministry and mission.

When I traveled to Israel recently, I passed a cemetery for "righteous gentiles." Oskar Schindler is buried there. You may have seen Steven Spielberg's Academy Award–winning film *Schindler's List* about Oskar Schindler's life (Universal 1993). Schindler was a terribly flawed human being—an alcoholic, gambler, and womanizer, a man driven by lust and greed. A German, he moved to Poland to profit from World War II. He lived in an apartment that had been confiscated from a Jewish family and opened a factory to make cookware for the German army. He supplied the factory with slave labor from concentration camps, people for whom he paid the Nazis.

Schindler's burning bush moment came one day when he was out with his mistress riding horses on a hillside overlooking the Jewish ghetto in Krakow, Poland. There he witnessed German soldiers brutally clearing out the ghetto and shooting people—young and old alike— who tried to run away. Suddenly Schindler found that he was no longer able to ignore the atrocities that were taking place. In an instant he went from Stage 1 to Stage 3, and his life changed. He exhausted all his resources and wealth in a single-minded effort that saved 1,100 Jews from the gas chambers and ovens. Oskar Schindler had discovered the purpose for which he was created.

Your life mission will always be connected to God's redemptive purpose, not your own self-interest. Moses' life mission grew out of his early experiences, but in the end it was an expression of God's will:

> Then the LORD said, "I have observed the misery of my people who are in Egypt; I have heard their cry on account of their taskmasters. Indeed, I know their sufferings, and I have come down to deliver them from the Egyptians . . . . The cry of the Israelites has now come to me; I have also seen how the Egyptians oppress them. So come, I will send you to Pharaoh to bring my people, the Israelites, out of Egypt." (Exodus 3:7-10 NRSV)

God does not invest in our personal agendas. He has called us to invest in his redemptive plan. Stage 1 is "Bless me." Stage 2 is "Save me." Stage 3 is "Use me."

Fully Present to God

I don't want to play at being the church; I want the real thing. I would rather die at age sixty-two knowing I have been about the work and purpose for which God sent me, than to live to age ninety asking what it was all about. No matter where we are on the ladder to God's dream—whether struggling with appetite, approval, or ambition—we can't take anything with us except what we have done for God. What you have done toward your unique God-purpose is the only thing that will live beyond your earthly existence.

Ask yourself as you finish this chapter: Which of these three life stages am I in right now? What am I praying? Is it God bless me, God save me, or God use me? Have you seen a burning bush? Do you feel you have heard from God about your BHAG, your Big Hairy Audacious God-purpose? If you have, then act on it! A dream without action is meaningless.

Maybe you're not sure about your God-purpose and are confused. You want to know God's dream for you but feel stuck. That is an okay place to be. Start by praying, "God, save me." Then make yourself available to the Lord by confessing, "God, I don't know what you want me to do, but I'm yours without reservation. Just show me, and use me. I am yours and you are mine." There are no do-overs in this life; we need to seize each moment to be fully present to God.

Building Your Life Mission Statement

Part 3

In building your life mission statement, use the following questions to evaluate where you have come from, so you can see more clearly where you are going.

- What struggles in your life have you had to overcome? How have those struggles defined you?

- God can use all things to strengthen his kingdom, and we are called to do the same. How can you share the lessons learned from your struggles?

- How have those lessons helped you in the past, and how might God use them to shape your future?

Notes

4

Lose Your Big Buts

But Moses said to God, "Who am I to go to Pharaoh and to bring the Israelites out of Egypt?"

God said, "I'll be with you. And this will show you that I'm the one who sent you. After you bring the people out of Egypt, you will come back here and worship God on this mountain."

(Exodus 3:11-12)

4

Lose Your Big Buts

Excuses, excuses—we all have them. "*But* I don't have the right kind of education." "*But* I'm too old to live that dream." "*But* the money just isn't there." "*But* that decision feels way too risky." "*But* I'm just one ordinary person."

Frankly, no dream worth pursuing will come easily. There will be obstacles, and there will be excuses—what I call our "big buts." If we are to fulfill God's dream for our lives, we have to lose our big buts, or at least downsize them.

As I mentioned, when I was a young pastor I was fortunate to be mentored by Christian business experts from around the country who wanted to help me and other young pastors develop systems that would provide a broader context for sharing the gospel. Ken Blanchard, probably best known for his book *The One Minute Manager*,[1] was one of the business people who helped us develop our life mission statements In a previous chapter, we looked at the three parts of my expanded life mission statement. However, Ken also recommended that each of us have an elevator statement, or a way of succinctly stating our mission in just one sentence or phrase. The elevator speech for my life mission statement became: To connect people to their God-destiny (i.e., To connect people to their burning bush).

A God-dream, or burning bush, is the "Aha!" moment when you realize, "Yes, this is what God wants me to do." You are then able to articulate it. For most of us, it isn't our day job. The Sudan Project is not my day job; but the Sudan started becoming a burning bush when I saw the juxtaposition of the sedan and Sudan in the local newspaper. The spark ignited by those images was not easily extinguished. I remember sitting in a cinema next to my wife and starting to weep during scenes from *The Constant Gardener*, about a Janjaweed militia attack in Darfur (Universal Studios, 2005). I watched *Hotel Rwanda*, a powerful true-life account from the Rwandan genocide of the early 1990s, when almost a million people were slaughtered over a horrific one hundred days (MGM, 2005). The fire within kept burning and getting hotter. The vision of God will burn inside of you and not go out. It will continually be rekindled.

A Boatload of Buts

Let's return to the story of Moses in Exodus 3. Moses had just had a God-vision, a burning bush experience. Moses was eighty years old, and God told Moses to leave the land of Midian and return to Egypt, where Moses would take on the Pharaoh and his armies and deliver tens of thousands of people from slavery. (Exodus 12:37 tells us the Israelites numbered at least 600,000, not counting the children.) As you can imagine, Moses came up with a boatload of "buts."

I'm Not Qualified

The first big but is in Exodus 3:11. "But Moses said to God, 'Who am I to go to Pharaoh and to bring the Israelites out of Egypt?'" In other words, "God, I'm not qualified."

Do you ever say that to God? Well, rest assured that if you *do* feel qualified, then your mission is not big enough. To put it another way, if you are only doing things you think you can accomplish, then you haven't discovered your life mission. God wants to challenge you and stretch you. God's true purpose for you probably will feel impossible. If that seems harsh, just remember: God said, "I'll be with you" (Exodus 3:12).

I'm Spiritually Unfit

The second big but is in verse 13: "But Moses said to God, 'If I now come to the Israelites and say to them, "The God of your ancestors has sent me to you," they are going to ask me, "What's this God's name?" What am I supposed to say to them?'" In other words, "But God, I'm spiritually unfit. I'm spiritually ill-prepared. I'm spiritually illiterate."

Many of us look at Moses and think he had it together—that he had an intimate relationship with God. But he didn't really know who God was. Think about it: For the first forty years of Moses' life, he was exposed to the pantheon of Egyptian gods, and as a prince of Egypt he would have been expected to study them all. Then for the next forty years of his life, Moses was in Midian, where his father-in-law was a priest; the Midianites were also polytheistic. Moses probably believed there were all kinds of gods, many of which he had studied and even worshipped. In essence he was asking God, "Which one are you? What am I supposed to tell the people when they ask me your name?"

As a pastor, I run into this type of excuse fairly often. I'll turn to someone in the congregation and say something like, "Have you ever thought of serving as a cell group leader?" More often than not, the person will respond, "I would, but I don't know enough about the Bible." In other words, they're saying, "I don't have this Jesus thing figured out for myself. How can I help someone else?" Let me tell you this: I have a master's degree and a doctorate in theology, and I still can't figure out the Trinity. If you can explain it to me, please get in touch.

Here is how God answered Moses' second big but: "I Am Who I Am" (v. 14). What kind of answer was that? It didn't really address Moses' question. However, it was what Moses needed to hear, because in essence God was saying, "Don't put me in a box." He was reminding Moses, as all of us need to be reminded, that an infinite God cannot be grasped by our finite minds. Too many times those of us in church sit back and think we have it all figured out. We know who's going to heaven, who's not, and why. But God is telling Moses, "I am too big to understand, but guess what? I am here with you. I am not uninvolved or impersonal. I see the injustices. I hear the prayers of my people. I am here to do something about it, and I am going to do it through you."

In my Jesus journey, I am at best an adolescent. All I know is that God looks like Jesus, and Jesus looks like God. In John 8:58, Jesus says, "I assure you...before Abraham was, I Am." (Abraham lived about two thousand years before Jesus.) What I know for sure is that I must continue humbly to submit myself and my thinking to Jesus. If I just keep following Jesus, then God's work will be displayed through my life. I don't have to be big enough for my life mission, because God is.

No One Will Believe Me

The third big but is found in Exodus 4:1. (By the way, notice the chapter number. Can you believe that when God put an amazing call on Moses' life, Moses spent two whole chapters arguing with God about it? He was never going to win that argument!) Moses asked God, "But what if they don't believe me or pay attention to me? They might say to me, 'The Lord didn't appear to you!'" In other words, "But God, what if I can't convince them? These people know who I am. I lack credibility."

I can relate. When I was a teenager, besides playing in a rock group that was busted for illegal drugs, I was also caught selling beer to minors. Of course, I was still a minor myself at the time. Then I found Jesus. Six months later, I started a Christian youth movement in my North College Hill neighborhood. It was the era of race riots in Cincinnati, and we were working on bringing black kids and white kids together. It was a powerful movement, but adults in the area said no one would trust me. They assumed, based on my past, that they knew all about me—that I was just looking for a new angle to make a few bucks or for new ways to get into trouble.

Moses also had a past reputation to worry about. Remember, he fled Egypt after murdering an Egyptian citizen. Moses believed if he went back, he would have all the credibility of a murderer. Moses, like all of us, doubted what God could accomplish through him. We base those expectations on our own understanding of our limitations and failures, and also on other people's opinions.

I remember when I told my mom and dad that I needed to go to college because God had called me into ministry. They were skeptical, as I mentioned before. Instead of believing me, they believed the high school guidance counselor who said I wasn't college material. After all, the guidance counselor was the expert. As a result, my mom and dad would not pay for college, which was a good thing because I had to go out and work. It helped me grow up and mature. So I paid my way through college and then went on to seminary, graduating in 1976. The high school counselor wasn't such an expert after all. Amazingly, one of my seminary professors still sends me words of encouragement every Sunday night. One of his recent emails gave a series of quotes that show just how wrong "experts" can be:

"*Gone with the Wind* is going to be the biggest flop in Hollywood."
—Gary Cooper, when he turned down the part of Rhett Butler[2]

"Fred Astaire can't act, can't sing, balding, can dance a little."
—MGM Studios[3]

"Try another profession, any other."
—Head instructor of the John Murray Anderson Drama
   School, to Lucille Ball[4]

"We don't like their sound. Groups of guitars are on their way out."
—Decca Records, referring to the Beatles before they were
   signed by Capitol Records[5]

I'm Afraid

The fourth big but can be found in Exodus 4:10. Moses told God, "My Lord, I've never been able to speak well, not yesterday, not the day before, and certainly not now since you've been talking to your servant. I have a slow mouth and a thick tongue." In other words, "I stumble over my words, Lord. I'm afraid to speak in front of people."

I'm an introvert, though given my current profession that may be hard to believe. I completely lost confidence in my public speaking when I was in the fifth grade. For Christmas Eve, the biggest night of the year at my church, they asked me to get up and pray during worship. I was to be joined by two other fifth graders, Jenny White and Carole West. Jenny and Carole were the "A" students. You know the type. Their job was to read the Christmas story as they stood on either side of me. When they were done, I was supposed to pray. When the big night came, Jenny read her part; then Carole read hers. But as Carole finished, I was frozen in place, caught like a deer in the headlights. After an awkward pause, Jenny elbowed me and whispered, "Pray!" I opened my mouth and said, "Now let us bow our hair in prayer." The adults struggled to contain their laughter, but Jenny and Carole didn't even try. They burst out laughing, and I was humiliated.

After that experience, I still can't believe that as an adult God has chosen me to speak. Jesus said there will be a time when all of us will be called to speak on his behalf. But he also said when that time comes, we will be given the words to say. In other words, it will not be us speaking but the Spirit of God, the Holy Spirit, speaking through us. This reliance on the Spirit is now what empowers me to do what I am called to do.

Drawing on God's Strength

I am not cured of being an introvert. After I preach, people often approach to chat, and they are surprised to find that I'm not the same guy I seemed to be during the sermon. The most I can usually conjure up in that situation is, "How are you?" and "Fine." I'm not good at small talk. But up on stage, God's strength is displayed through my weakness. God's power is shown through my inadequacy. Look at God's response to Moses in Exodus 4:11: "Who gives people the ability to speak? Who's responsible for making them unable to speak or hard of hearing, sighted or blind? Isn't it I, the LORD?"

Moses appeared to be totally inept and inadequate for the mission God had called him to. So, why did God choose him? And why does God choose you or me? Eugene Peterson, a pastor who wrote the paraphrase of the Bible called *The Message*, said,

> But maybe that's the point. Salvation is God's work: Jesus saves. Incompetence may be the essential qualification, lest we impatiently and presumptuously take over the business and start managing a vast and intricate economy that we have no way of comprehending.[6]

Don't you love that? Humbly, rather than capably. Incompetence may be the essential qualification.

When Saddleback Church pastor Rick Warren was asked to appear as Oprah Winfrey's guest on her program *Lifeclass*, he made his appearance conditional on one request: he wanted to bring a friend to appear on the show with him. I watched the show and was blown away. Rick's friend was Nick Vujicic, a guy who should cause all of us to lose our big buts.

Nick was born in Melbourne, Australia, in 1982—without arms or legs, the result of a congenital disorder called tetra-amelia syndrome.

Nick had a tough time as a child, often experiencing discrimination and bullying, until it reached the point where at age ten he tried to kill himself. He survived, and when he grew closer to God as a teen, he realized he wasn't the only person in the world with severe disabilities. With that realization, he learned to embrace his lack of limbs in order to inspire others. Even though he has no legs, Nick has two small feet, one of which has two toes. Using what he has been given, he has learned to type on a computer, take care of himself, golf, swim, and even skydive. As an evangelist, motivational speaker, and founder of a nonprofit organization called Life Without Limbs, Nick is living out his God-dream, to inspire others and draw them closer to God. I encourage you to search YouTube for Nick Vujicic and Oprah Winfrey to watch the story that I found so captivating. You'll realize, as I did, that there are no big buts left, not after you give your life to Jesus Christ.

In Romans 12:2, Paul reminds us to do what Nick did: "Don't be conformed to the patterns of this world, but be transformed by the renewing of your minds so that you can figure out what God's will is—what is good and pleasing and mature." Many of us give our lives to the Lord Jesus Christ, but we keep the same old thoughts. In order to bring about what you were created for and do all God wants to do through you, there has to be a renewing of your mind.

Naysayers

Excuses aren't always something we come up with on our own. Sometimes we claim self-limiting beliefs that are assigned to us by others. What self-limiting beliefs do you need to shed? "He's not college material." "She doesn't have the talent for that." "She isn't the right color (or creed or age)." We've got to be careful who we listen to! Naysayers limit our goals and create fear that at worst is paralyzing and at best prevents us from living out the fullness of God's dream for our lives. An event later in Moses' story provides a great example of how listening to the wrong folks can create fear, paralysis, and excuses for not living out our God-dream.

About a year after Moses led the Israelites out of Egypt, he sent twelve people ahead of everyone else to check out the Promised Land. He said:

> "Go up there into the arid southern plain and into the mountains. You must inspect the land. What is it like? Are the people who live in it strong or weak, few or many? Is the land in which they live good or bad? Are the towns in which they live camps or fortresses? Is the land rich or poor? Are there trees in it or not? Be courageous and bring back the land's fruit." (Numbers 13:17-20)

In other words, Moses was directing this select team to go into the land and serve as the architects of God's preferred future.

Jumping ahead to verse 27, we see that the people came back with a report that met Moses' expectations: "We entered the land to which you sent us. It's actually full of milk and honey, and this is its fruit." If they had only stopped there! But ten of the twelve people (all but Joshua and Caleb) continued their report in verses 28-33.

> "There are, however, powerful people who live in the land. The cities have huge fortifications. And we even saw the descendants of the Anakites there. The Amalekites live in the land of the arid southern plain; the Hittites, Jebusites, and Amorites live in the mountains; and the Canaanites live by the sea and along the Jordan . . . .The land that we crossed over to explore is a land that devours its residents. All the people we saw in it are huge

men. We saw there the Nephilim (the descendants of Anak come from the Nephilim). We saw ourselves as grasshoppers, and that's how we appeared to them."

As a result of that negative report, the children of Israel became afraid and wandered the desert for another thirty-nine years.

Be careful who you listen to! So often when God plants a God-dream in our mind, there is a prophet of gloom and doom who comes along and says, "Yes, but." Have you ever met these "Yes, but" types? I have, which is why I work hard to develop a network of people around me who sing the possibilities of God's promises. I don't have time for negative people. I'm sorry; I just don't.

Besides being careful who you listen to, be careful what you say. During that thirty-nine-year period, hundreds of thousands of Israelites died in the wilderness as a result of ten people's negativity and the fear it fostered. That's why my life rule is: speak faith when you feel futility. This doesn't mean the road to God's dream will be easy. The future doesn't just stand there waving us in.

The Flag of God's Promise

Miracles often are wrapped in opposition. When I came to Ginghamsburg Church as a young pastor and declared, "God is going to touch the world from this little church," I experienced opposition. The godfathers and godmothers of the church stood up, shook their heads, crossed their arms, and said, "Over our dead bodies." Well, not to be mean about it, but through the years God has arranged that.

I don't want to be one of the ten who waved the white flag of surrender. I want to stand with Joshua and Caleb, the two who lifted the flag of God's promise and said in Numbers 13:30: "We must go up and take possession of it, because we are more than able to do it."

To live the dream, we must do what God is telling us now. We must fully possess the rights and privileges we have in Christ Jesus today, not risk the dream with our own big buts or those that others try to impose upon us.

Before we move on, let's spend some time on next steps for developing our life mission statements.

Building Your Life Mission Statement

Part 4

There is a huge difference between an obstacle and an excuse. An obstacle is something to work through, over, or around, whereas an excuse stops you in your tracks.

- What tightly held excuses prohibit you from living God's dream for you?

- Excuses aren't always something we come up with on our own. Sometimes we claim self-limiting beliefs assigned to us by others. From what self-limiting beliefs do you need to break free?

- Becoming clear about your life mission statement means chopping away at excuses to follow the purpose God has for you. Take some time and write a prayer asking God to remove your excuses. List your excuses in the prayer.

Notes

5

What Is in Your Hand?

The LORD said to him, "What's that in your hand?"

Moses replied, "A shepherd's rod."

The LORD said, "Throw it down on the ground." So Moses threw it on the ground, and it turned into a snake. Moses jumped back from it. Then the LORD said to Moses, "Reach out and grab the snake by the tail." So Moses reached out and grabbed it, and it turned back into a rod in his hand. "Do this so that they will believe that the LORD, the God of their ancestors, Abraham's God, Isaac's God, and Jacob's God has in fact appeared to you."

(Exodus 4:2-5)

5

What Is in Your Hand?

When Moses encountered his burning bush, it exposed his lack of confidence and his perception of his own resources as limited. But then God asked him a question that became the catalyst for all the resources Moses could ever possibly need. It's time for us to lay hold of the same confidence and provision as we ask ourselves that very same question: what is in your hand?

I hope you have been working on your life purpose and eliminating your "big buts." Psalm 139 declares that every one of us has been intricately woven together in our mother's womb, fearfully and wonderfully made. God has a purpose for each of us, and we have been created with everything needed to fulfill that purpose. Life is short. We will soon stand before God on Judgment Day, and I want all of us to be able to say, "Father, I have finished the work that you sent me to do." We just have to realize that everything we need, we already have.

Seeing with God's Eyes

I have shared my three-part mission statement with you, which includes equipping church leaders to reach future generations. One way I do this is by teaching master's and doctoral degree seminary classes for students from around the country. I also speak at conferences nationally and internationally. Ginghamsburg has served as a teaching church for over twenty years, bringing in pastors and church leaders from around the world for training and conferences. As time permits, I also work with a team to create books and video resources to help leaders develop self-leadership, discipline, and tools for taking the church into the world in missional ways.

The primary course that I teach for master's degree students is held in Ginghamsburg's original small country church building, located about a mile down the road from our current primary campus. The first thing I ask my students to do is explore the building, inside and out. Constructed in 1876, it's a modest little place. The neighborhood is modest, too, consisting of a couple of dozen houses. No real estate agent would feature them in an advertisement. Cars on cinder blocks are a neighborhood staple, along with a trailer park, chickens wandering across the road, and never-ending yard sales.

I ask my students, "If you were seeing this place for the first time and didn't have the advantage of hindsight, what picture would you have developed for its God-potential? What would you do if you were sent to pastor this church?"

I didn't choose to come to Ginghamsburg. Our United Methodist bishop sent me there. He told me thirty-five years ago that if I did a good enough job, in two or three years I could move to another church. I came to an inadequate facility with a minuscule budget in an obscure location. To make matters worse, the area has declined in population the entire time I have been here. Yet today, Ginghamsburg is one of the largest United Methodist churches in the country, despite the challenge of not being located near a thriving urban center.

We downsize our dreams when we only look through human eyes, seeing obstacles, personal limitations, and a perceived lack of resources. A God-dream is an impossible dream because *you* can't do it; God does it through you. When I arrived at Ginghamsburg Church, I could have limited my vision of its potential based on what I saw with my physical eyes. Instead, I decided to believe in a God who sees things not as they are but as they will be.

The story of Gideon in Judges 6 is a great example. As the chapter opens, the Israelites in the days before King Saul and King David had managed as usual to turn their backs on the God who had delivered them out of slavery and into the Promised Land. For seven years they had been oppressed by the Midianites, who had repeatedly burned the Israelites' crops and killed or taken their livestock. In other words, all their means of income and support had been taken from them. God, as in the days of Egyptian slavery, was fully aware of their plight and planned to do something about it, this time through a little-known guy named Gideon.

The Lord's angel appeared at Gideon's side in Judges 6:12, declaring, "The LORD is with you, mighty warrior!" Through the angel, God went on to say, "You have strength, so go and rescue Israel from the power of Midian. Am I not personally sending you?" (v. 14). Like Moses at the burning bush, Gideon was skeptical: "With all due respect, my Lord, how can I rescue Israel? My clan is the weakest in Manasseh, and I'm the youngest in my household" (v. 15). Instead of hearing what the Lord God had called him to do, the "mighty warrior" Gideon couldn't get past his own perceptions of smallness and limitation. He was looking through human eyes, not God's eyes. But God persisted, telling Gideon, "Because I'm with you, you'll defeat the Midianites as if they were just one person" (v. 16).

When I first discerned God's call at Ginghamsburg, I could have said, "Who, me? A skinny youth pastor from Cincinnati who almost failed high school? And by the way, God, have you gotten a good look at this place?" I could have downsized the dream to what I thought I could do, not what God could and would do through me.

Don't fall into that trap! Dreaming God-sized dreams is part of the Holy Spirit's work in our lives. Remember that God promised on Pentecost that the Holy Spirit would be given to all people, as prophesied in Joel 2 and declared by Peter in Acts 2. And *all* in the Greek means—you guessed it—*all*.

Using What We Have

Let's return to Exodus 4, where we were examining Moses' burning bush experience. Moses was eighty years old when he learned his mission through the burning bush; thank God he discovered it before he died! Moses ran through his litany of "big buts," but God wasn't about to let him off the hook.

Then, in Exodus 4:2, God asked Moses the critical question: "What's that in your hand?" Moses answered, "A shepherd's rod"— basically a staff, a stick. You know that Moses had to be thinking, "What am I going to do with a stick?" After asking the question, the Lord gave a command: "Throw it down on the ground" (v. 3). So Moses threw it on the ground. It became a snake! What did Moses do? He "jumped back from it"; in other words, he ran or at least thought of running. Looking at our own lives, how often do we run from the work that God is trying to accomplish through us? But God wasn't through with Moses yet:

> Then the LORD said to Moses, "Reach out and grab the snake by the tail." So Moses reached out and grabbed it, and it turned back into a rod in his hand. "Do this so that they will believe that the LORD, the God of their ancestors, Abraham's God, Isaac's God, and Jacob's God has in fact appeared to you." (v. 4-5)

Now, the problem is that you and I tend to focus on what we don't have versus what we do have. Please hear me: in God, everything that you need you have already been given. In God, all the resources required to accomplish the mission you were created for you already possess. God uses our ordinary gifts, talents, and life experiences, which you and I often take for granted, to fulfill his dream for us.

What was the shepherd's staff? It was an ordinary tool that Moses used every day. The terrain where he tended sheep was hazardous and hilly, and at times he used the staff to brace himself and keep from slipping off the mountainside. The staff also served as a weapon if there was an attack by robbers or predators such as hyenas or wolves. The crook or curved end of the staff was used to guide the sheep, which I imagine at times could be almost as difficult to herd as cats. The shepherd would slip the crook around a sheep's neck, and since there were no sharp edges it didn't hurt the animal. As soon as the sheep felt the crook, it would be startled and would stop. Then the shepherd could gently move the sheep wherever he wanted it to go. The staff might also be used at night to carry a lantern when it was dark on the narrow paths or when the camp needed to be lit. There was no way Moses could conceive how that simple shepherd's staff would be used to fulfill God's mission. It would ultimately intimidate a Pharaoh, part a sea, lead people through a wilderness, and bring water from a rock.

Like Moses, we often are oblivious to the simple tools we can use to fulfill God's purposes. As I write this, I'm thinking about my computer keyboard, which I use daily to write and answer email. It's an amazing tool when you think about it, though I don't completely understand how it works. I don't even have to think about where the letters are; my fingers automatically go there. (My little finger is especially familiar with the delete key, because I have to use it a lot.)

It's amazing how God uses our simple tools and the collective weight of all our life experiences, even failures, to fulfill our life purpose. Think about it: Moses became a shepherd through failure. It was quite a fall to go from prince to pasture. Shepherds were on the lowest rung of society, but God used that failure for his redemptive purpose. And it wasn't only Moses' shepherding experience that would come in handy; it was all his life experience. Acts 7:22 tells us, "Moses learned everything Egyptian wisdom had to offer, and he was a man of powerful words and deeds." Notice that it doesn't say he had learned all the Scriptures. So, why was he useful to God? Moses knew how to infiltrate the Egyptian culture. He was a student of his contemporary culture and had mastered it.

Picture a seed. It contains all the genetic code needed to create what it will become. Have you ever visited the giant trees in Sequoia National Park? The genetic code for those gigantic trees came from one seed. Similarly, one human embryo contains all the DNA needed to create a mature human being. So if God has woven into you all the gifts, talents, and DNA you need to get the job done, then what is the Holy Spirit's part?

I was thinking about this the other day as I was passing winter wheat fields. In Ohio where I live, winter wheat is typically planted around October. After a week or two in the ground, it begins to grow. But then, in the cold and freezing winter weather, it goes dormant and starts to turn brown, much like grass in the wintertime. It then waits for the warming of the soil in spring to awaken from its dormancy.

Okay, what does this have to do with you? The Holy Spirit is the warmth of the spring soil that awakens these latent gifts and talents in you. That is what happens in our new birth. We are given the Holy Spirit, and the Holy Spirit awakens our gifts and talents. It's what Scripture means when it says, "For you were dead, but now you have new life" (Romans 6:13 NLT). We must learn to submit to the Holy Spirit and say, "Holy Spirit, I give you my mind, my thoughts. I surrender my mouth, my speech. I give you my hands that they may serve your every purpose. I give you my feet that I only go and follow wherever Jesus leads."

The more you surrender to the Holy Spirit, the more powerful God's influence becomes to use your gifts and talents in the world. Everything you need, you have already been given.

Head, Hands, Heart

Are you scratching your head, unsure as to which gifts and talents you have and are supposed to use? Three key questions will help you identify them.

The first question is: "What are the gifts of my head?" In other words, what do you know a lot about? What do you know more about than a lot of people around you? Let me share one example from my own life.

As a kid I was forced to go to church, and I observed a great deal about why church didn't relate to unchurched people. It was behind-numbingly boring! I loved what the wider culture had to offer. I enjoyed the music and movies; I liked to hang out in clubs. Even today I struggle to listen to Christian radio stations because the music seems to be so boring. It repeats over and over again, "We love you, Jesus" and "Thank you, Jesus, for loving us." Now, all of that is certainly true, but it is delivered in a manner that can feel trivial and trite. From an early age I knew and understood why the church felt irrelevant to the unchurched. I really got it. And I used that head knowledge as a pastor to avoid being that kind of church.

The second question to ask is: "What are the gifts of my hands?" What do you do better than a lot of people around you? The one thing I did really well, even as a kid, was to start new things that would grow and attract other people. When I was a junior in high school, I played guitar in a rock band. I have a picture of me performing that year at a high school dance. I am not too hard to pick out: I am the only white face in the crowd. Being in that band gave me the idea to start a club where teens could come and dance. I found a place, opened a club, and started making up to eighty dollars a night. Back in the 1960s that was a lot of money for a sixteen-year-old kid. I had a talent for starting new things that would attract people and even make money. Do you see how God used this? What God awakened in my life was the ability to start things that would grow and attract people to come and join in the rhythm of God's big dance.

God was also working on something else in my life at the same time—my drive to stand up and speak out against racism, sexism, and any other "ism" that divides or denigrates. The race riots of 1968 had a huge impact on my life and my future understanding. Do you see how God can use all your experiences and the gifts of your hands?

The third question is: "What is the passion of my heart?" I was most passionate about connecting students to Jesus Christ. If Jesus could change our lives, he could change our high school. And if he could change our high school, he could change our community. And if he could change our community, he could change our world.

That passion is still burning. Burning bushes don't go out. Every year, I return to my alma mater, North College Hill High School in Cincinnati, to hold assemblies. Carolyn and I give a few scholarships each year to high-potential students.

Those three questions will help you discover what is in your hand: What are the gifts of my head? What are the gifts of my hands? What is the passion of my heart?

I love to see how the people in my church answer the questions. One of those people is Jim Sitzman. Jim is good at figuring out how to fix stuff. I asked him about it, and he shared that his dad owned a mobile home park and would take Jim with him to maintain homes and equipment. Jim's dad was handy and never had to hire a contractor, so Jim learned a great deal just by following his dad around. Jim now uses that head knowledge, as well as the gifts of his hands, to lead our car ministry. He can fix cars that everyone else has given up on. He has been at it for eighteen years and estimates the ministry has given at least six hundred cars away and repaired six hundred more. The gifts of his head and hands have combined with the passion of his heart—providing people in need, especially single moms, with safe, reliable transportation—to create his calling in life. And because of his passions, others have been drawn in to serve alongside Jim.

We are born for and wired for a God-purpose in the world. God's question to you is: "What is in your hand?" Everything you need has already been given to you. Then, as with Moses and his staff, God commands you to throw it on the ground. Think about that for a minute. It's a strong directive. God didn't say, "Why don't you gently place it on the ground?" Many times we think, "Maybe I won't really throw it. I'll just keep my hand on it, in case this doesn't work out." I hear people say many times, "Well, I knew I was not supposed to sit around and only take. I knew I was supposed to move out and do. But then it got a little risky and cost more money or time than I thought." With that kind of thinking, we snatch the gift or talent back out of God's hand again because we never really released it for his purposes. Throwing it down is a definitive action. As a matter of fact, the literal translation of Exodus 4:3 means, "Make or take up a challenge." It is a commitment to join an enterprise. Through the years and across cultures, similar expressions have developed like "throwing down the gauntlet" and "throwing my hat in the ring." It is a bold and definite action.

I love this quote, often attributed to Thomas Edison: "Vision without implementation is hallucination."[1] If Jim Sitzman had never started the car ministry, if he had taken back the gift, then 1,200-plus people would never have been blessed.

As you answer the three questions for yourself, you might discover a plethora of resources in your own life that you were completely unaware of. Are you old enough to remember the TV show *The Beverly Hillbillies* from the 1960s? It was about a man named Jed Clampett who was living in poverty on top of an oil field because he didn't recognize it was there. That is what so many of us are doing as Christians. We are living in spiritual poverty, when just beneath it we have the power of the Holy Spirit and an array of gifts just waiting to be activated by the Spirit.

Release It to Increase It

Once you recognize what is in your hand, you then have to release it to increase it. You have to take what you have been given by God and release it into God's hand. Then you don't take it back again until God tells you to do so. When God does put it back in your hand, it's no longer just a stick; it's God's stick.

One January, I had a very humbling experience. Ginghamsburg, like all churches and nonprofits, was scrambling to generate and mail all the giving statements for the previous year so that people had the information to do their income taxes. Of course, we had to do this for all our campuses, including the two in Dayton that were in at-risk and socioeconomically challenged communities. However, two statements wound up on my desk that couldn't be mailed to Dayton attendees. Here's why. The only address we had for those folks was "Homeless." It shocked me. Here were people who did not have a place to live but were giving back to God. Last time I checked, we had 1,800 families in our congregation who gave nothing. Am I, are you, is any one of us going beyond the tithe in our giving? Are we giving out of the fullness of our blessing? These people were giving out of their poverty.

Thinking doesn't create energy; action creates energy. We can't think our way into a new way of acting. We have to act our way into a new way of thinking. Sometimes people approach me and say, "Mike, I would like to get going; I would like to do stuff, but I'm having intellectual problems with what I read in the Bible. It's hard to commit to it." I know it's hard. I struggle with faith. But I'm not sitting around trying to think my way into a new way of acting. I just keep moving.

Ron Will is a member of our church and works as a subcontractor at a U.S. Air Force base. As Ron was sitting in worship a number of years ago, he was meditating about his burning bush, his life mission, and he thought about the problem of addiction in our culture. Without asking for financial help from the church, he founded two houses in Dayton that provided badly needed residency programs for addicts, and he called it Joshua Recovery Ministry. Last year at the church's leadership board retreat, we were praying about how

God wanted to direct some of the small pool of money that remained from the previous year's Christmas Miracle Offering. One member suggested that we support Joshua Recovery Ministry, and the board quickly agreed, unbeknownst to Ron. Soon a check for $10,000 was in the mail. Ron sent me a thank-you note a short time later. He said, "Mike, we have men living in two different houses. We were down to $17.50 in our checking account until that $10,000 check came in."

At the beginning, when you choose your life mission, you may not have all the ingredients you think you need for success. They will come at the appointed time. Just release what is in your hand, throw it down for God's purposes, and don't look back. Acting by faith on God's promise is the only resource you need. When you give your best, you can trust God with the rest.

Building Your Life
Mission Statement

Part 5

Take a moment to examine the gifts God has given you. If you have trouble answering these questions, find people in your life who know you well and ask for their help.

- What are the gifts of my head?

- What are the gifts of my hands?

- What is the passion of my heart?

Notes

6

Perseverance

"The eye is the lamp of the body. Therefore, if your eye is healthy, your whole body will be full of light. But if your eye is bad, you whole body will be full of darkness. If then the light in you is darkness, how terrible that darkness will be! No one can serve two masters. Either you will hate the one and love the other, or you will be loyal to the one and have contempt for the other."

(Matthew 6:22-24)

6

Perseverance

As we read on in Exodus, we can see that Moses' God-dream was not going to be a walk in the park. But *quit* was not in his vocabulary. What about yours? What will become of your God-dream when obstacles appear? And trust me, they will.

I hope as you have worked through the previous chapters that you have started to discern your life mission statement. If you are still struggling, then perhaps it will help to look at some examples from members of Ginghamsburg Church:

My life mission statement is to end the feeling of inadequacy, isolation, and confusion people feel during a medical crisis, through communicating what I know, using the resources I have, and advocating for families and individuals through the process.

My life mission is to connect with the younger generation so that they aren't afraid of religion and start to turn away from it, to help them find their way back.

My life mission statement is to seek and develop opportunities to teach, mentor, guide, and develop relationships with retirees and retirement age members and attendees of Ginghamsburg Church.

My life mission is to organize life groups to serve people in need by providing one-day home improvement services.

My life mission is to help children through the pain of neglect, feeling unloved, and living through the struggles of sexual abuse.

My mission is to end slavery, especially in sex trafficking. I want to use the strengths of strategic planning to grow funding and awareness for Ohio's link in the worldwide trafficking network. But, I also want to use my strengths to enhance and develop the local programs that build self-worth for sexually abused women.

These are excellent life mission statements. For most people, however, identifying the mission may be the easy part. The hard part is dealing with the frustration that comes along the way. After teaching about this, I am often approached by people who have developed life mission statements but aren't happy about the setbacks they are experiencing on the journey. So, let's be clear. No truly God-sized dream will be fulfilled immediately. It will have setbacks and frustrations. The question is: What do we do when those challenges arise? What separates those who *do* from those who *don't*?

A Sustaining Vision

Turn with me to Deuteronomy 34, the last chapter in the Bible about Moses' life. Recall that by that time, Moses had had his burning-bush experience as an eighty-year-old man and had accomplished what seemed to be an impossible mission: go to Egypt and deliver the people of Israel from bondage. In Deuteronomy 34 we jump ahead forty years. Start in Deuteronomy 34:1-3 (NIV):

> Then Moses climbed Mount Nebo from the plains of Moab to the top of Pisgah, across from Jericho. There the LORD showed him the whole land—from Gilead to Dan, all of Naphtali, the territory of Ephraim and Manasseh, all the land of Judah as far as the Mediterranean Sea, the Negev and the whole region from the Valley of Jericho, the City of Palms, as far as Zoar.

Moses was now 120 years old, but he was still receiving a big vision from God. Many of the people I know who are age sixty and up are looking backward and doing less. Yet at the time of his death, Moses continued to have a forward focus. Now look at verses 4-7:

> Then the LORD said to him, "This is the land I promised on oath to Abraham, Isaac and Jacob when I said, 'I will give it to your descendants.' I have let you see it with your eyes, but you will not cross over into it." And Moses the servant of the LORD died there in Moab, as the LORD had said. He buried him in Moab, in the valley opposite Beth Peor, but to this day no one knows

where his grave is. Moses was a hundred and twenty years old when he died, yet his eyes were not weak nor his strength gone.

What separates those who *do* from those who *don't*? We find the key in that final verse. When the Bible refers to Moses' eyes, it doesn't mean his physical eyes; it means his focus and ultimate priority. Moses was successful in his God-dream because he had a sustaining vision.

This is what Jesus meant when he talked about making blind eyes see: bringing vision to the lost, giving them and us the clarity to focus on the "one thing," the God-priority. Keeping this in mind helps to provide context as we read what Jesus had to say in Matthew 6:22-24 (CEB) during his Sermon on the Mount:

> "The eye is the lamp of the body. Therefore, if your eye is healthy, your whole body will be full of light. But if your eye is bad, your whole body will be full of darkness. If then the light in you is darkness, how terrible that darkness will be! No one can serve two masters. Either you will hate the one and love the other, or you will be loyal to the one and have contempt for the other."

Your eyesight, your vision, has to have a clear focus, without distraction, on the one thing, the God-thing. Many of us are too easily distracted; then the picture gets fuzzy, and dreams start to feel unachievable. Jesus pointed out that we can't serve two masters without winding up hating the one and loving the other.

Why is the sustaining vision so critical? Proverbs 29:18 tells us: "When there's no vision, the people get out of control." In other words, if you don't remain focused on your life mission, then you will lack the discipline to complete it. This is what separates success from failure, and those who do from those who don't. We need to have a process for renewing and sustaining that vision.

Go to the Mountains

Mountains in Scripture always signify a place to go in order to get a clearer vision. Moses' first burning bush started on a mountain when he was eighty years old. (By the way, if you're eighty years old and reading this book, you're on the right track. It's not too late to define your God-dream. If you haven't done it yet, it's time to start today!) At the time of Moses' death forty years later, he was still seeking mountains. His final vision was from Mount Pisgah.

If you study Moses' life in its entirety, you will see that he often retreated to the mountains to receive the sustaining word of God that would fuel his mission. Sometimes he would go into the mountains for forty days at a time. In the Gospels, you will also notice that Jesus, after a long day of teaching or healing, would often retreat to the mountains to sustain his vision. Now, in my sixties, I see that this practice is absolutely critical. No matter how young or old you are, you must maintain a future focus. You must always seek God's preferred future. Too many of my friends have started looking toward retirement. Then they start dwelling on bygone accomplishments. Anytime you begin looking to the past, it means death. You might as well hang it up. Even at age 120, Moses maintained a future focus.

Before I came to Ginghamsburg in April 1979, I had been an associate pastor in Cincinnati. When my mom saw the country church I had been sent to, she was upset. She didn't think that her son had pursued his master's degree just to end up at some tiny chapel. I had been serving as the youth minister in a big church in Cincinnati, where there were lots of kids, a gymnasium, a game room, and many other extras. I was going from that to a two-room country church!

When the district superintendent called me about my new pastoral appointment, he asked me to meet him for dinner at a hotel in a neighboring town because he refused to tell me where he was sending me before we met. He said it would depress me. Later, when he first brought us to visit Ginghamsburg and to see the building, my wife was ready to head back to Cincinnati. But I sensed a burning bush within myself saying, "No, God is going to do a great work through this place."

During my first spring at Ginghamsburg, I spent an entire day in the field behind that little country church, asking God what his vision was for the place. As I left the field, I was picturing three thousand people in worship. So I went to my superintendent and said, "Guess what? There are going to be three thousand people who worship in this place!" His response? "Mike, I appreciate your youthful enthusiasm, but the biggest church in Ohio has never had more than twelve hundred in attendance, and it's in Cincinnati." Twelve hundred in worship had become the ceiling of people's picture of possibility.

In looking through God's eyes, I was able to glimpse a day when that little church would be a faith movement that was engaging its community and its world, helping to meet the needs of both. What I saw on that day in the field was a diverse, inclusive church of all races and economic groups. (Let me tell you, if it's all white, it ain't right! That applies to the foods we eat as well as to the churches we attend.) I saw a teaching church that, through conferences and seminars, would empower other churches in America and around the world to come and see what God can do in out-of-the-way places with ordinary people.

Every August, it's been a tradition for Carolyn and me to have a visioning retreat, in which we go away to dream God's dream. Sometimes we go to physical mountains, other times to metaphorical mountains. Regardless, we are constantly looking over the next mountain to God's preferred future. About ten years ago during our visioning retreat, I felt the inner voice of the Spirit say to me that Ginghamsburg's ministry was not about building the biggest church in the area but about churching the area. That vision was part of the impetus for our two urban campuses in Dayton.

I kept looking out further, and in August of 2004, God opened my eyes to the humanitarian crisis in Sudan. Since 2005, Ginghamsburg Church and its partner churches and schools have started 243 schools serving 29,000 students, most of whom are Muslim. We have established sustainable agriculture and safe water programs. We have built health clinics in South Sudan that are serving thousands and have trained community healthcare workers.

In my August 2012 visioning retreat, I saw the importance of live-streaming worship on the Internet and envisioned how many more people we could reach. The following January I took our senior leadership team to the mountains to begin working on a succession plan because I'm not getting any younger. I will keep serving and dreaming God's dreams until I die, but who is going to be God's Joshua or Deborah to follow me in this particular part of my mission?

I tell you these things not to draw attention to Ginghamsburg or to compare our mission with Moses' mission. I do it to say: Keep going. Keep trying. Persevere. When you get tired of dealing with the obstacles, go to the mountains. Talk to God. Listen for his vision, and don't be afraid to change.

Setbacks and Frustrations

Moses experienced a multitude of setbacks and frustrations. He went to Pharaoh nine times, yet Pharaoh said he would not let the slaves go free. Pharaoh finally got so upset that he said to Moses in

Exodus 10:28, "Get out of here! Make sure you never see my face again, because the next time you see my face you will die." Seems like most people would have gotten the message right then and there. So, what did Moses do? He went back a tenth time.

Moses' setbacks weren't just because of Pharaoh. They came from the Israelites, the very people he had helped. After finally leaving Egypt, they would whine to him, "Oh, Moses! Manna every day! Manna for breakfast, lunch, and supper! We're tired of manna, Moses! How about some meat? How about some chicken? And by the way, the water is terrible. Moses! Moses! Moses!" Do you know people like that? I certainly do.

The first six months after Carolyn and I came to Ginghamsburg, the resistance was painful. A group in the congregation had organized an initiative to get rid of us and called a church meeting. They had written letters to the bishop asking to have us removed. People stood up and said all kinds of cruel things. Some said they were used to older pastors, and here was this twenty-seven-year-old kid with long hair and blue jeans telling them what to do. One guy asked me, "Since you came from the city, how can you understand rural people?" Another stood up in church, shook his finger at me, and said, "Young man, we've been here for a long time, and we'll be here long after you're gone!" Well, as it turns out, I am still here—and he isn't.

Moses had a "no-quit" perseverance, and so must we. Here is one of my favorite quotes, from the American writer Robert Louis Stevenson: "Saints are sinners who kept on going."[1] A friend of mine from a nearby town would certainly agree. He says to me, "Slaughter, I can't understand why people are so interested in what you are doing. I've watched you for thirty-five years, and during any one year you have not done anything great. You just don't go away!"

Apparently I'm in good company. Thomas Edison developed the first long-burning light bulb. It would burn for fifteen hundred hours at sixteen watts. In developing the light bulb, Edison persevered through three thousand different theories before he found one that worked. He tested six thousand types of fiber for carbon filament before he found success. He said, "Many of life's failures are people who did not realize how close they were to success when they gave up."[2] Whoa! Saints are sinners who keep going.

Albert Einstein agreed. He once said, "It's not that I'm smart, it's just that I stay at problems longer."[3] Years ago, Carolyn and I visited the house in Vienna where Beethoven, who had lost his hearing by that time, wrote his Ninth Symphony. To this day I wonder how you can be deaf and write something like the Ninth Symphony. Ray Charles was blind, and so is Stevie Wonder. James Earl Jones, a wonderful actor who among other roles voiced Darth Vader in *Star Wars*, is a stutterer. (Lucasfilm, Twentieth Century Fox 1979–83). President Franklin D. Roosevelt was paralyzed from polio. And yet all these people persevered.

Perseverance also means remembering who resources our mission. We don't need to have all the resources at the outset of our mission to accomplish what God is calling us to do; the resources will be given at the appointed time. Look at Moses! He set out from Egypt with a city-worth of people and headed into the wilderness. (And there is always a wilderness; any God-sized dream has to pass through the testing grounds of the desert.) When Moses set out to lead the masses, he didn't wait until he had all the supplies. He didn't rent U-Haul trucks, or figure out how much food they would need for forty years—no, he stepped out.

Here is my philosophy of life: ready, fire, aim. (Saying that always makes my staff and wife cringe a little bit.) Too many people say:

"Ready, aim, fire." If you do that, given the speed of our world today, you may miss out. Moses set out, and what did God do? God provided the resources one day at a time. Notice that if the people became fearful and hoarded God's provision instead of releasing it, the manna rotted. They may have been in an arid desert, but God brought water from a rock. Here is what separates success from failure and those who do from those who don't: Successful people have a way of renewing and sustaining the vision so that it is not consumed; it does not burn out or run out.

Heaven's Legacy

What our lives come down to can be embodied in one word: *legacy*. Our life mission is what will live beyond us. Look at Deuteronomy 34:5-6 (NIV) with me again:

And Moses the servant of the LORD died there in Moab, as the LORD had said. He buried him in Moab, in the valley opposite Beth Peor, but to this day no one knows where his grave is. Moses was a hundred and twenty years old when he died, yet his eyes were not weak nor his strength gone. The Israelites grieved for Moses in the plains of Moab thirty days, until the time of weeping and mourning was over.

At that time the people went back to partying. This is exactly how it is. I've buried a lot of people as a pastor. We come together and have the funeral, people say a few nice things, we drive to the cemetery, and then we all come back to the church and eat potato salad. People party; people forget. In a hundred years, no one is going to remember you and me. No one is going to know where we are buried because it's not about us. It's really not even about our legacy. It's about heaven's legacy.

Jesus said in Matthew 28, just before he ascended to heaven, "I've received all authority in heaven and on earth." That comes from pretty high up; that is something we need to pay attention to. He then said, "Therefore, go and make disciples." That is part of all our missions. Each of us will play it out differently, but all of us are called to go and make disciples of Jesus Christ for the transformation of the world.

Look at what God said to Abraham in Deuteronomy 34:4 (NIV), "This is the land I promised on oath to Abraham, Isaac and Jacob when I said, 'I will give it to your descendants.' I have let you see it with your eyes, but you will not cross over into it." The word *descendants* reminds us that the most important mission all of us have is to make sure our children, grandchildren, and future generations will enter God's place of promise.

Always remember: our children will become who we are, not what we say. As parents, we need to be aware of our compromises. Where have we bought into the values of our society? Where have we allowed our vision to become clouded? We miss church for a soccer game. We skip youth group because of private lessons. Worshipping God is a priority for us and our children. The Word reminds us to "train children in the way they should go; when they grow old, they won't depart from it" (Proverbs 22:6).

Follow the example of Moses, who trained Joshua, his successor:

Now Joshua son of Nun was filled with the spirit of wisdom because Moses had laid his hands on him. So the Israelites listened to him and did what the LORD had commanded Moses. (Deuteronomy 34:9 NIV)

Who are you investing in right now? Who are your Joshuas? Remember, we are all called to be God-connectors, both within our own and future generations.

One of my favorite movies is *City Slickers* (Castle Rock Entertainment 1991). Billy Crystal's character Mitch—a New York City businessman, husband, and father having a midlife crisis— is trying to "find himself" by vacationing at a dude ranch. I love the scene where a crusty old cowboy named Curly, played by Jack Palance, turns to Mitch and asks, "Do you know what the secret of life is?" Of course, Mitch doesn't have a clue. Curly holds up one finger and says, "This." Mitch asks, "Your finger?" Curly replies, "One thing, just one thing." Mitch immediately asks, as we all would, "What's the one thing?" Curly grins and tells him, "That's what you gotta figure out."

Have you figured out your one thing? Are you prepared for the distractions and detractors? Will you persevere? Just remember, in moments of darkness never doubt what God has promised you in the light.

Father God, I am so thankful that you never let us go, in our distractions, in our false priorities, in our failures. Lord, clear our vision and renew our focus. Give us the courage to persevere. Amen.

Building Your Life Mission Statement

Part 6

In the previous chapters, you've laid the foundation for your life mission statement:

Chapter 1: Name people and qualities you admire.

Chapter 2: Identify needs in your neighborhood, community, and world.

Chapter 3: Look back at your struggles and how they define you.

Chapter 4: List excuses that prevent you from living God's dream.

Chapter 5: Claim your gifts of head, hands, and heart.

Now that the foundation is in place, it's time to build your life mission statement. Remember:

- This is not your mission; it's your part of God's mission.

- It's not just for this year or even five years; it's for your whole life.

- The mission should be challenging and may even seem impossible. That means you're on the right track.

- You may need to draft several versions of the statement, now and later.

- Once you have a long version, try writing a short "elevator" version to use in sharing the statement with others.

One of the best resources available is your community. Take the rough draft or final copy of your life mission statement and share it. Use your life group, co-workers, or Facebook as a test audience.

Notes

Epilogue

You are going to die. I am one hundred percent certain of it, unless Jesus decides to come back in your lifetime. Life is an incredible gift, but people receive it in different ways: some people are doers, and other people are watchers. One of my favorite doers in the Bible is Peter, a screwup like me, who often didn't get it right but was determined to be in on the action—not benched on the sideline.

The classic example from Peter's life is in Matthew 14. Jesus had been praying on a mountainside, getting reconnected with his mission after a long day of teaching, healing, and—oh, yes—feeding five thousand. In the meantime, Jesus had sent his disciples by boat across the lake to their next destination. A strong headwind kicked up in the middle of the night, and the boat, with the disciples on board, was battered and beaten by the waves. The disciples, already frightened by the storm, spotted a man walking on the water toward them. From a distance they were convinced he was a ghost, but as he drew near, the man called out and said he was Jesus. Peter, being Peter, boldly asked if he could join Jesus. "Lord, if it's you, order me to come to you on the water" (v. 28). Jesus replied, "Come" (v. 29). So, Peter jumped out and started walking. He was doing great until he looked at the waves beneath his feet. He lost his nerve and started to sink, at which time Jesus extended a hand.

One of the things we can see in Peter's example is that doers aren't immune from fear. The difference is that they act on it anyway. Yes, Peter started sinking, but sinking isn't failing. The eleven who stayed in the boat let fear get the best of them. Doers know there are no comebacks, no do-overs. Life is short. Notice Peter's motivation for jumping out of the boat. He might have put it this way: "Lord, if you are in it, I want to be a part of it. I don't have enough time in this short lifetime to do *my* thing; I want to do yours—to walk where you walk and work where you work."

As you may have noticed by now, pursuing the dream often means suspending logic. Logic can be your enemy. Walking on water isn't logical. Think about the Wright brothers. It didn't seem logical that something heavier than air could remain airborne for any length of time. Legend has it that at the very moment they were making their first manned flight on a beach in North Carolina, a physics professor in Europe was lecturing that flight wasn't humanly possible.

You and I live, not by sight but by faith. Our worldview is defined by the Resurrection, and resurrections don't make sense! They're not logical. And yet Jesus said, "All things are possible for the one who has faith" (Mark 9:23). Pursuing your God-dream means understanding that the real basis for reality is not what you see, but the force of the unseen Creator behind it. When you understand that, you realize anything is possible.

Look back at the story of Peter and the boat. Jesus told him, "Come," and Peter responded.

Jesus is the Son of God, resurrected from the grave. He is creator of the universe. He is Lord, with a capital *L*, which means he has absolute authority. When he beckons to you and says, "Come," how will you respond? "Tomorrow"? "Maybe some other time"?

No! Get out of the boat! You will experience the miracle God made for you when you hear and obey what Jesus is saying in your life. That's the difference between a daydream and a God-dream. A God-dream happens when you put perspiration to inspiration.

I am living my God-dream, and there is nothing sweeter. I want that for you. Today, I want you to choose to live and die for your dream—not with it. Amen.

Notes

Prologue
1. John 17:4

Chapter 1. Dreaming the Dream
1. Jim Collins, *Good to Great: Why Some Companies Make the Leap and Others Don't* (New York: HarperCollins, 2001), 190.
2. C. S. Lewis, *The Chronicles of Narnia* (New York: HarperCollins, 2001), 86.
3. http://www.upenn.edu/almanac/between/2004/commence-b.html.

Chapter 2. Discovering Your Birthright
1. Associated Press, "U2's Bono Joining Venture Capital Firm," June 15, 2004, USA Today, http://usatoday30.usatoday.com/life/people/2004-06-15-bono-venture-capital-firm_x.htm.
2. Rick Warren, *The Purpose Driven Life* (Grand Rapids: Zondervan, 2002).
3. Charles Colson, *Loving God* (Grand Rapids: Zondervan, 1997), 24.

4. To learn more about God's financial plan for your life, check out my book *shiny gods: finding freedom from things that distract us* (Nashville: Abingdon, 2013).

Chapter 3. Your Burning Bush
1. Martin Luther King Jr., "I've Been to the Mountaintop," April 3, 1968, http://mlk-kpp01.stanford.edu/index.php/encyclopedia/documentsentry/ive_been_to_the_mountaintop/
2. Martin Luther King Jr., *The Autobiography of Martin Luther King, Jr.*, Clayborne Carson, ed. (New York: Warner Books, 1998), http://mlk-kpp01.stanford.edu/index.php/kingpapers/article/chapter_1_early_years/

Chapter 4. Lose Your Big Buts
1. Kenneth H. Blanchard and Spencer Johnson, *The One Minute Manager* (New York: William Morrow, 2003).
2. http://www.imdb.com/title/tt0031381/trivia.
3. A&E, "Fred Astaire," http://www.biography.com/people/fred-astaire-9190991.
4. Tom Cor, ed., *The 2,320 Funniest Quotes: The Most Hilarious Quips and One-Liners from Allgreatquotes.com* (Berkley: Ulysses, 2011), 144.
5. Editors of Publications International, Ltd., "9 Bits of Irony," September 20, 2007, HowStuffWorks.com, http://www.howstuffworks.com/9-bits-of-irony.htm.
6. Eugene H. Peterson, *Christ Plays in Ten Thousand Places: A Conversation in Spiritual Theology* (Grand Rapids: Eerdmans, 2005), 152.

Chapter 5. What Is in Your Hand?
1. As quoted by Daniel A. DiBiasio in his inaugural address at North Ohio University, http://www.onu.edu/node/38084. However, the quote is also attributed to Benjamin Franklin.

Chapter 6. Perseverance

1. A quote often attributed to Robert Louis Stevenson, http://www.reference.com/motif/health/famous-quotes-about-never-giving-up.
2. http://www.goodreads.com/author/quotes/3091287.
3. http://www.getinspired365.com/20130314.

Dare to Dream
Churchwide Study

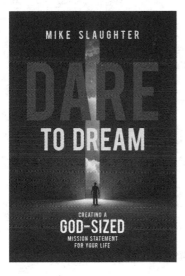

*D*are to Dream is a startling and inspiring new series that draws on the Bible and a lifetime of ministry to help us discern God's dream for us and learn to live it out prayerfully and enthusiastically.

The series includes videos and readings for each week, with directed questions for discovering and creating your life mission statement. The six-week study contains a complete family of resources for the entire church.

DVD
ISBN 978-1-4267-7578-9

Youth DVD
ISBN 978-1-4267-7582-6

Leader Guide
ISBN 978-1-4267-7579-6

Youth Book
ISBN 978-1-4267-7580-2

Children's Leader Guide
ISBN 978-1-4267-7581-9

Preview Book
ISBN 978-1-4267-7583-3

Abingdon Press™

Christmas Is Not Your Birthday

Every year, we say we're going to cut back, simplify, and have a family Christmas that focuses on the real reason for the season—Jesus. But every year, advertisements beckon, the children plead, and it seems easier just to indulge our wants and whims.

This Christmas, cut through the hype that leaves you exhausted and broke at the end of the year. In five short, engaging chapters, pastor Mike Slaughter will inspire you to approach Christmas differently and be transformed in the process.

ISBN 978-1-4267-2735-1

A Different Kind of Christmas
Churchwide Study

Help your church cast a vision of living and giving like Jesus, beginning with the Christmas season and continuing through the year. This five-week churchwide study, based on Mike Slaughter's popular book *Christmas Is Not Your Birthday*, helps participants see past the traps and discontentment of consumerism to discover God's call to live generously in fulfilling God's mission in the world.

The comprehensive resource includes videos from Mike Slaughter; studies for adults, youth, and children; and 28 days of devotions for Advent and Christmas.

DVD
ISBN 978-1-4267-5354-1

Leader Guide
ISBN 978-1-4267-5363-3

Devotions
ISBN 978-1-4267-5360-2

Youth Study Edition
ISBN 978-1-4267-5361-9

Children's Leader Guide
ISBN 978-1-4267-5362-6

shiny gods:
finding freedom from things that distract us

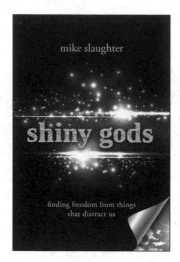

In a culture guided by shiny, life-promising distractions, "enough" seems elusive and keeps us chasing the next quick fix.

What if the Giver of Life offered freedom from this downward spiral—would you take it? In *shiny gods*, pastor and author Mike Slaughter helps readers reassess priorities to create a culture and lifestyle of giving, based on the Word of God and the example of Christ. In his book, DVD, and leader guide, Slaughter helps us consider these topics:

- Naming Our Idols
- Money, Work, and Debt
- Be Faithful, Save, and Give
- Heart Giving

Book
ISBN 978-1-4267-6194-2

DVD
ISBN 978-1-4267-6201-7

Leader Guide
ISBN 978-1-4267-6196-6

AVAILABLE WHEREVER FINE BOOKS ARE SOLD.

FOR MORE INFORMATION ABOUT MIKE SLAUGHTER, VISIT WWW.MIKESLAUGHTER.COM.

first:
putting GOD first in living and giving

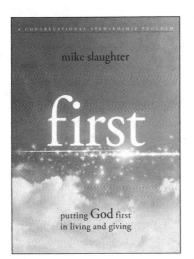

What happens when we truly put God first in all aspects of our lives? In *first: putting GOD first in living and giving*, pastor and author Mike Slaughter conducts a four-week all-church stewardship program to help participants create a culture and a lifestyle of faithful living and giving. This stewardship program is based on Slaughter's popular book, *shiny gods: finding freedom from things that distract us.*

The *first* program kit includes the *shiny gods* book, DVD, and leader guide, plus one each of the *first* program components: program guide with flash drive; devotional book; youth study edition; and children's leader guide.

Program Kit
ISBN 978-1-4267-7573-4

Program Guide with Flash Drive
ISBN 978-1-4267-6554-4

Devotions
ISBN 978-1-4267-6202-4

Youth Study Edition
ISBN 978-1-4267-6363-2

Children's Leader Guide
ISBN 978-1-4267-6368-7

Abingdon Press™

AVAILABLE WHEREVER FINE BOOKS ARE SOLD.
FOR MORE INFORMATION ABOUT MIKE SLAUGHTER, VISIT WWW.MIKESLAUGHTER.COM.

Change the World:
Recovering the Message and Mission of Jesus

Something is not working. Despite the church's place of prominence in American culture and the ubiquity of the church in every American town, misconceptions about the faith of Jesus Christ run rampant today. Christians are known more for exclusivity than for love, more for potlucks than for solving world hunger.

It's time for churches to get over the cruise-ship mentality of being program providers, and reconnect with the true message and mission of Jesus—to bring good news to the poor, release to the captives, and freedom to the oppressed.

ISBN 978-1-4267-0297-6

Abingdon Press™

AVAILABLE WHEREVER FINE BOOKS ARE SOLD.
FOR MORE INFORMATION ABOUT MIKE SLAUGHTER, VISIT WWW.MIKESLAUGHTER.COM.

Momentum for Life:
Biblical Practices for Sustaining Physical Health, Personal Integrity, and Strategic Focus

Visionary pastor Michael Slaughter calls all aspiring leaders to a life of faith, balance, and purpose. Operating on the principle that all leadership begins with self-leadership, the book outlines five crucial disciplines:

- **D**evotion to God
- **R**eadiness for lifelong learning
- **I**nvesting in key relationships
- **V**isioning for the future
- **E**ating and **E**xercise for life.

Readers will gain insights and advice for enriching the spiritual, intellectual, interpersonal, missional, and physical areas of their lives, all of which are integral to effectiveness as a leader.

ISBN 978-0-687-65009-5

UnLearning Church

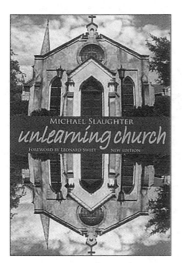

How many things does your church do just because that's the way it's always been done? Does your congregation value tradition over passion and stability over creativity? If so, it's time to unLearn. Leading congregations into a dynamic and prophetic future requires unLearning what you thought you knew about the church, leadership, and life.

Pastor Michael Slaughter casts a vision for innovative and authentic congregations, and for the kind of leadership that can bring congregations to greater vitality and impact in today's postmodern culture. Readers will be challenged to gaze boldly beyond franchised church models to a dynamic embodiment of God's unique vision for each leader and each congregation.

ISBN 978-0-687-64708-8

AVAILABLE WHEREVER FINE BOOKS ARE SOLD.
FOR MORE INFORMATION ABOUT MIKE SLAUGHTER, VISIT WWW.MIKESLAUGHTER.COM.